MARKET MINDS: STOCK MARKET PSYCHOLOGY

The stock market has long been an enigma to many. For some, it represents a world of endless opportunities, where fortunes are made overnight. For others, it embodies a place of fear, where investments are gambled, and financial ruin is a constant threat. Both of these perspectives often exist in the minds of traders and investors simultaneously, fluctuating as frequently as the price charts they study. While understanding technical indicators, financial reports, and market trends are crucial for success, an often overlooked yet critical component is stock market psychology.

Many novice investors enter the stock market with a purely logical approach: buy low, sell high. It seems simple enough on the surface. However, anyone who has ever tried to implement this strategy knows that it's far from straightforward. The financial markets are not solely driven by rational decision-making. They are influenced by emotions, biases, herd mentality, and even cognitive errors that traders make without realizing. Understanding the human psychology that underpins market movements is essential for mastering the art of investing.

At its core, stock market psychology deals with how traders and investors react to financial news, price movements, and market trends. It explores the influence of emotions such as fear, greed, anxiety, and euphoria on decision-making. The volatility of markets often triggers emotional responses that can drive irrational behavior, leading to both missed opportunities and catastrophic losses.

Understanding and mastering stock market psychology requires more than simply acknowledging the impact of emotions. It calls for a deep dive into the psychological mechanisms that affect decision-making, awareness of cognitive biases, and the development of strategies that counteract the negative influence of emotional trading.

The stock market is a complex, dynamic system influenced not only by economic data and financial fundamentals but also by the collective psychology of its participants. To succeed, investors must go beyond the technical aspects of trading and develop an understanding of their own psychological tendencies.

Mastering stock market psychology does not mean eliminating emotions altogether; that's impossible. Instead, it's about developing the self-awareness, discipline, and strategies needed to make more rational, informed decisions. Those who can control their emotions, overcome their biases, and remain disciplined during times of market turbulence will have a significant edge over those who cannot.

In the end, while knowledge and skill are vital components of trading success, the real differentiator lies in the mind. Embrace the psychological challenges of the stock market, and you'll find yourself better prepared to navigate its ups and downs with confidence.

THE MIND OF THE MARKET

The stock market is often perceived as a complex mechanism where numbers, algorithms, and economic indicators govern trading decisions. Yet, despite the rise of sophisticated technology and quantitative analysis, human emotions continue to play an integral role in shaping market outcomes. Traders, investors, and even financial institutions are subject to the forces of fear, greed, optimism, and uncertainty. This article delves into the intricate relationship between emotions and stock market behavior, explaining how psychological factors can lead to market volatility, bubbles, crashes, and trends.

Before diving into specific emotions, it's important to understand the broader concept of behavioral finance, a field that combines psychology and finance to explore why people make irrational financial decisions. Traditional finance theories, such as the Efficient Market Hypothesis (EMH), assume that markets are rational and that all available information is reflected in stock prices. Behavioral finance, however, challenges this by acknowledging that cognitive biases and emotional responses can lead to decisions that deviate from logic.

Psychological factors, particularly emotions, influence how individuals interpret information, assess risk, and make investment choices. Two key emotions that stand out in financial markets are fear and greed, but others like excitement, frustration, and overconfidence also play a significant role.

In the world of finance, two powerful emotions—fear and greed—often dictate the decisions made by investors and significantly influence market trends. These emotions are deeply embedded in human nature and have been a driving force in markets since the dawn of trade. While many investors may believe that their choices are purely based on logic and sound analysis, fear and greed have a way of infiltrating even the most disciplined mind, leading to irrational behaviors, herd mentality, market bubbles, and sudden crashes.

Understanding how fear and greed shape market behavior is crucial for both individual investors and financial institutions. By recognizing these emotional forces, market participants can make more informed decisions, avoid common psychological pitfalls, and better navigate the volatile waters of the financial markets.

Fear and greed are the two primary psychological forces that influence investors. Both emotions are fundamental to human survival, as they have helped individuals navigate threats and opportunities throughout history. In the financial markets, these emotions take on a unique form, affecting how people perceive risk, reward, and uncertainty.

Greed plays a critical role in driving bull markets, speculative bubbles, and individual investment decisions that may appear overly optimistic. While greed is not inherently negative—it is part of what motivates people to invest in the first place—excessive greed can lead to unsustainable market conditions and, eventually, market crashes.

Greed is the desire for financial gain and is often associated with taking excessive risks in pursuit of greater rewards. In the context of the stock market, greed manifests as the motivation to buy more assets in the hopes of making larger profits, sometimes ignoring the inherent risks involved. When greed dominates, investors may chase high returns, speculate on overhyped assets, or engage in short-term trading strategies that lack a solid foundation.

While greed drives market rallies and bubbles, fear is the force behind market downturns, corrections, and crashes. Fear can have a paralyzing effect on investors, leading them to avoid risk altogether or, worse, to sell their holdings in a panic during a market sell-off.

Fear, on the other hand, is the emotional response to the possibility of loss. It drives people to avoid or minimize risk. In financial markets, fear can manifest as panic selling, where investors rush to sell their holdings to prevent further losses. When fear takes over, it can lead to irrational decisions, such as selling stocks at the bottom of a market downturn or avoiding potentially profitable investments due to anxiety about future risks.

Both emotions are at odds with each other, but they work together in a cyclical pattern, creating market trends, bubbles, and crashes. Investors constantly oscillate between the two emotions, and this balance between fear and greed helps explain why markets move the way they do.

Greed is perhaps the most prominent emotion that affects market behavior. It represents the desire for financial gain, often leading investors to take excessive risks in pursuit of higher returns. Greed can manifest in various ways, including:

Chasing Hot Stocks: Investors driven by greed often flock to stocks that are experiencing rapid price increases, hoping to capitalize on short-term gains. This can lead to market bubbles, where asset prices soar far beyond their intrinsic value.

Speculation: Greed drives speculative behavior, where investors make bets on the future direction of prices without solid evidence or fundamental analysis. They might invest in overhyped sectors or technologies, hoping for outsized returns.

Leveraging Investments: To amplify potential profits, investors may borrow money to invest more heavily in the market. This leverage can result in enormous gains when the market moves in their favor but can also lead to catastrophic losses when the market turns.

Historically, many of the stock market's biggest bubbles have been fueled by greed. The tech bubble of the late 1990s, for instance, was a period marked by extreme speculation on dot-com companies, many of which had little revenue or profitability. Investors were captivated by the promise of the internet revolution and poured money into companies based on optimistic projections rather than solid financials. As the bubble burst in 2000, many of these investors lost significant amounts of capital.

One of the key psychological underpinnings of greed in the markets is the "greater fool theory." This theory suggests that investors are willing to buy overvalued assets because they believe they will be able to sell them to someone else at an even higher price—the "greater fool." This mentality is prevalent during periods of market euphoria, where the focus shifts from the intrinsic value of assets to speculation on short-term price movements.

Greed also leads to individual investment decisions that prioritize short-term gains over long-term stability. Investors chasing high returns may gravitate towards riskier assets, such as volatile stocks, speculative startups, or high-leverage financial products like options and futures. The desire for outsized profits can cloud judgment, leading investors to ignore the risks associated with their investments.

For instance, during periods of low-interest rates, investors might seek higher yields by investing in junk bonds or other high-risk securities. While these investments can offer higher returns, they also carry a greater risk of default or loss.

Greed can push investors to overlook these risks in pursuit of higher profits, often leading to significant losses when market conditions change.

Fear is the counterbalance to greed and is responsible for many market downturns and crashes. When fear takes hold of investors, it can lead to panic selling, which in turn can drive stock prices lower and create a downward spiral. Common fear-driven behaviors include:

Flight to Safety: In times of uncertainty or economic distress, investors often move their money into "safe-haven" assets like gold, U.S. Treasury bonds, or cash. This causes a sell-off in riskier assets like stocks, pushing their prices lower.

Herding Behavior: Fear can lead to herding, where investors follow the actions of others rather than making independent decisions. If large groups of investors start selling off assets, others may feel compelled to do the same, exacerbating the decline in stock prices.

Exaggerating Negative News: Fear tends to amplify negative news, leading investors to overreact to developments that may not have long-term significance. For instance, a temporary economic slowdown or political uncertainty might result in sharp stock market declines, even if the fundamental health of the economy remains intact.

Panic selling occurs when fear overtakes rational decision-making, causing investors to sell their assets en masse. This behavior is often triggered by negative news, such as economic downturns, political instability, or corporate scandals. Fear spreads quickly in the market, especially in today's interconnected financial system, where news travels instantly through social media, news outlets, and financial networks.

Euphoria is the emotional high that often precedes a market bubble. When investors collectively feel overly optimistic, they tend to push stock prices to unsustainable levels, convinced that the market will continue to rise indefinitely. During periods of euphoria:

Overvaluation: Stocks become significantly overvalued as investors focus on potential future gains rather than current fundamentals. Metrics like price-to-earnings ratios skyrocket, and some companies are valued based on little more than hype.

FOMO (Fear of Missing Out): The fear of missing out is a key driver during euphoric markets. Investors who might otherwise be cautious feel pressured to buy into the market because they see others making money. This herd mentality drives prices even higher.

The Greater Fool Theory: During market euphoria, some investors rely on the belief that they can always sell their overvalued assets to a "greater fool" willing to pay an even higher price. This speculative attitude further inflates the bubble.

When fear turns into panic, markets can enter a freefall. Panic occurs when investors, convinced that the market is about to collapse, rush to sell off their holdings at any price. This can result in steep declines in stock prices, even when the underlying fundamentals remain relatively unchanged.

The interplay between fear and greed creates a cycle that drives market trends. Markets tend to move in cycles, alternating between periods of growth (bull markets) and decline (bear markets). These cycles are not only influenced by economic factors but also by the emotional responses of investors.

Capitulation is the point at which investors give up entirely, selling their assets regardless of the loss they might incur. This is often seen as the bottom of a market crash, as it represents the final wave of selling before the market begins to stabilize.

Beyond raw emotions like fear and greed, several cognitive biases also influence how investors behave in the stock market. These biases often lead to irrational decision-making, contributing to market inefficiencies. Some of the most common cognitive biases include:

Overconfidence Bias: Investors may overestimate their ability to predict market movements, leading them to take excessive risks. Overconfidence can cause traders to ignore warning signs and hold onto losing positions for too long.

Confirmation Bias: Investors tend to seek out information that confirms their pre-existing beliefs while ignoring data that contradicts their views. This can lead to poor decision-making, especially during volatile market conditions.

Loss Aversion: Loss aversion refers to the tendency to feel the pain of losses more acutely than the pleasure of gains. As a result, investors may hold onto losing positions for too long, hoping for a rebound, or sell winning positions prematurely to lock in profits.

Anchoring Bias: Investors often anchor their decisions to a specific piece of information, such as the price they paid for a stock or a target price. This can lead to irrational decisions when new information suggests a change in strategy. These biases, combined with the emotional swings of the market, contribute to inefficiencies that can create opportunities for savvy investors.

Given the influence of emotions on stock market behavior, various sentiment indicators have been developed to help investors gauge the collective mood of the market. These indicators provide insight into whether the market is driven by fear, greed, optimism, or pessimism. Some commonly used sentiment indicators include:

The VIX (Volatility Index): Often referred to as the "fear gauge," the VIX measures expected market volatility based on options trading. A high VIX indicates elevated fear, while a low VIX suggests a calm market.

Put/Call Ratio: This ratio compares the volume of bearish put options to bullish call options. A high put/call ratio indicates a bearish sentiment (fear), while a low ratio suggests a bullish outlook (greed).

Investor Surveys: Various surveys, such as the American Association of Individual Investors (AAII) sentiment survey, track whether investors are feeling bullish, bearish, or neutral about the market.

Breadth Indicators: These indicators look at the number of advancing versus declining stocks. A market with broad participation across many sectors suggests optimism, while narrow participation indicates caution.

By monitoring these indicators, investors can get a sense of whether the market is in a state of fear, greed, or somewhere in between, helping them make more informed decisions. While emotions often lead to irrational short-term market behavior, long-term investors can benefit by maintaining a disciplined, emotion-free approach. Some key strategies for avoiding emotional decision-making include:

Diversification: A well-diversified portfolio can help reduce the emotional impact of market swings. By spreading investments across different asset classes and sectors, investors can mitigate the risk of significant losses in any one area.

Dollar-Cost Averaging: This strategy involves regularly investing a fixed amount of money into the market, regardless of its current condition. By consistently buying shares over time, investors can reduce the emotional pressure of trying to time the market. Dollar-cost averaging helps smooth out the impact of volatility and prevents investors from making impulsive decisions based on short-term market movements.

Focus on Fundamentals: Long-term investors should prioritize the fundamental value of their investments rather than being swayed by short-term price fluctuations. This involves looking at factors such as earnings growth, cash flow, and the overall health of the business. By keeping a focus on these fundamentals, investors can avoid being swept up in the emotional tides of the market.

Stay Informed, But Not Overwhelmed: It's important for investors to stay informed about the market and the economy, but obsessing over daily market news can lead to emotional decision-making. Long-term investors can benefit from reviewing their portfolios periodically rather than reacting to every piece of news or short-term price movement.

Have a Plan and Stick to It: Developing a clear investment strategy, including setting goals, risk tolerance, and time horizon, can help investors stay disciplined during periods of market volatility. Having a plan in place reduces the likelihood of making emotionally driven decisions and ensures that investors remain focused on their long-term objective

In today's fast-paced, technology-driven world, the role of media and social networks in amplifying emotions cannot be overstated. The proliferation of financial news outlets, real-time stock data, and social media platforms has created an environment where information — and misinformation — spreads quickly. This constant barrage of news can intensify investors' emotional responses and lead to more pronounced market movements.

Media Hype: Financial media outlets often focus on sensational headlines and dramatic market movements to capture viewers' attention. Headlines like "Market Crash!" or "Record Highs!" can provoke emotional reactions, driving investors to buy or sell based on short-term news rather than long-term strategies.

Social Media and Herding: Platforms like Twitter, Reddit, and online forums have become influential in shaping market sentiment. For example, in 2021, retail investors using

Reddit's "WallStreetBets" forum famously drove up the price of GameStop stock, creating a short squeeze that cost hedge funds billions of dollars. This episode highlighted how quickly emotions like excitement, FOMO, and defiance can spread across social media, leading to extreme price movements.

Algorithmic Trading and Emotional Feedback Loops: Algorithmic trading, which uses automated systems to execute trades based on predetermined criteria, is becoming increasingly common. While these systems are designed to be emotion-free, they can inadvertently exacerbate emotional market reactions. For example, if a large sell-off occurs due to fear, algorithms might detect the downward momentum and trigger additional selling, creating a feedback loop that amplifies the market's emotional response.

Given the significant role emotions play in stock market behavior, emotional intelligence is a valuable skill for investors. Emotional intelligence refers to the ability to recognize, understand, and manage one's own emotions, as well as the emotions of others. In the context of investing, EQ can help investors stay calm during periods of market volatility and avoid making impulsive decisions.

Investors with high emotional intelligence are more likely to:

Stay Disciplined: Rather than reacting to short-term market movements, emotionally intelligent investors stick to their investment strategy and remain focused on their long-term goals.

Avoid Herding Behavior: By recognizing the emotional drivers behind market trends, emotionally intelligent investors are less likely to follow the crowd and can make more rational, independent decisions.

Manage Stress: Market downturns can be stressful, but investors with high EQ are better equipped to handle the psychological toll of market volatility. They understand that market fluctuations are a natural part of investing and are less likely to panic during downturns.

Developing emotional intelligence requires practice and self-awareness. Investors can improve their EQ by learning to identify their emotional triggers, practicing mindfulness, and staying informed about cognitive biases that influence decision-making.

The stock market is as much a psychological battlefield as it is a financial one. Emotions like greed, fear, euphoria, and panic can have a profound impact on market behavior, driving bubbles, crashes, and everything in between. While it's impossible to eliminate emotions from investing, understanding their influence can help investors make more rational decisions and avoid common pitfalls.

By staying disciplined, focusing on long-term goals, and developing emotional intelligence, investors can navigate the ups and downs of the market more effectively. Whether it's avoiding the temptation to chase a hot stock or resisting the urge to sell in a panic, recognizing the emotional forces at play is key to becoming a successful investor.

In the end, the stock market is driven by people, and people are inherently emotional. Understanding this dynamic is crucial for anyone looking to achieve long-term success in investing.

HERD MENTALITY: FOLLOWING THE CROWD

Herd mentality in the stock market refers to the phenomenon where individuals in the market make investment decisions based on the collective actions of others rather than independent analysis. This behavior, while rooted in evolutionary survival mechanisms, can have profound implications for the financial world. Understanding the psychology behind herd mentality in the stock market provides valuable insights into how markets behave during periods of volatility, bubbles, and crashes. In this exploration, we'll delve into the psychological drivers, historical examples, and consequences of herd behavior, as well as strategies investors can use to avoid falling prey to its traps.

Herd behavior has deep evolutionary roots, linked to survival instincts. Early humans survived by sticking together—whether hunting or escaping predators, being part of a group increased their chances of survival. Moving in herds allowed individuals to rely on collective wisdom, reducing personal risks. These instincts still influence modern behavior, including financial decisions.

In the context of investing, people tend to feel safer when they follow the crowd. When uncertainty strikes, trusting the actions of others offers psychological comfort, even when individual analysis suggests otherwise. This "safety in numbers" instinct creates the basis for herd behavior in the stock market.

One of the core psychological drivers of herd mentality is the concept of social proof, first popularized by psychologist Robert Cialdini. Social proof refers to the tendency of individuals to mimic the actions of others when they are unsure of what to do. In stock markets, social proof can be seen when investors base their decisions on what they observe others doing rather than on independent research. This often happens when there's uncertainty or a lack of clear information about the direction of the market.

Investors might reason, "If everyone else is buying, they must know something I don't." Social proof can trigger a feedback loop, leading to massive price movements as more people join the herd. The result is a self-perpetuating cycle: the more people invest in a particular stock or market trend, the stronger the validation becomes for others to follow.

The fear of missing out, or FOMO, is another psychological factor that drives herd mentality. Investors, particularly during a bull market or a speculative bubble, become anxious when they see others profiting from rising stocks or market trends. This fear can lead to impulsive, emotion-driven decisions as individuals rush to invest, fearing they will miss out on potential gains if they don't act quickly.

FOMO often overrides rational analysis and long-term thinking, leading to herd-like behavior. Investors may buy stocks at inflated prices simply because others are doing so, without considering the fundamentals. Once caught in this cycle, herd mentality can fuel market bubbles.

On the flip side, loss aversion—the tendency to prefer avoiding losses rather than acquiring equivalent gains—can lead to herd behavior during market downturns. Behavioral economists, including Nobel laureate Daniel Kahneman, have demonstrated that losses hurt more than gains feel good. In the stock market, this can lead to panic selling when prices begin to drop.

As investors see others selling, the fear of further losses grows, leading them to sell off their assets as well. This creates a downward spiral in prices. The more people sell, the more prices fall, which then induces more investors to join the selling wave. This negative herd mentality can lead to market crashes, with stocks often plummeting far beyond their intrinsic value.

One of the cognitive biases that exacerbate herd mentality in the stock market is confirmation bias. This bias leads investors to seek out information that confirms their preexisting beliefs or opinions, while ignoring or undervaluing information that contradicts them. In a herd context, once an investor sees others buying or selling a stock, confirmation bias may lead them to focus only on news or data that supports the prevailing trend. This selective information processing reinforces herd behavior and encourages investors to follow the crowd rather than critically evaluate the situation.

Anchoring bias occurs when investors rely too heavily on the first piece of information they receive when making decisions. In a volatile market, the actions of early movers (those who buy or sell large volumes of stock) can act as an anchor for subsequent investors. If influential figures or institutions start buying a particular stock, others may anchor their expectations around that initial action and follow suit, even if subsequent information suggests the stock is overvalued or risky.

The bandwagon effect is closely related to herd mentality and refers to the tendency for individuals to adopt a behavior because others are doing it, regardless of their own beliefs or analysis. In stock markets, this can lead to investors blindly following trends, jumping on the "bandwagon" of a popular stock or market sector without fully understanding the underlying risks. The more people join the trend, the more validation others feel in doing the same.

Herd mentality can also be reinforced by overconfidence bias, where investors believe they are better than average at predicting market movements. In a rising market, overconfidence can lead investors to assume they have unique insights, causing them to join the herd without fully considering the downside risks. Overconfident investors often fail to recognize that they are simply following the crowd, which can lead to exaggerated price movements and bubbles.

Herd mentality is a key driver of market bubbles and crashes. When investors collectively chase after rising assets, they often inflate prices far beyond their intrinsic value. This creates unsustainable bubbles, which inevitably burst when market sentiment shifts. The resulting crashes can lead to significant financial losses, not only for individual investors but also for the broader economy.

Herd behavior contributes to market volatility. When large numbers of investors follow the crowd, price movements become exaggerated, leading to sharp swings in stock prices. This volatility can make it difficult for long-term investors to navigate the market and can lead to widespread uncertainty and panic.

Herd mentality often results in the misallocation of capital, as investors pour money into overhyped assets while ignoring more fundamentally sound investments. This can distort market signals and lead to inefficient use of resources, with potentially long-lasting negative consequences for economic growth.

One of the most effective ways to avoid falling prey to herd mentality is to do independent research. Relying on personal analysis, rather than following the crowd, allows investors to make informed decisions based on facts and fundamentals. Investors should critically evaluate the reasons behind any market trend and consider whether it aligns with their own investment goals and risk tolerance.

Diversification is another powerful tool for mitigating the risks of herd mentality. By spreading investments across a variety of asset classes, industries, and geographies, investors can reduce their exposure to market bubbles and crashes. Diversification helps prevent overconcentration in any one stock or sector, reducing the likelihood of significant losses during periods of herd-driven volatility.

Adopting a long-term investment perspective is essential in avoiding the pitfalls of herd mentality. Markets can be incredibly volatile in the short term, especially when driven by mass psychological trends like fear, greed, or speculation. However, over the long run, markets tend to revert to their true value based on fundamental factors such as corporate earnings, economic growth, and interest rates.

Investors who focus on long-term goals are less likely to be swayed by short-term market fluctuations and the crowd's behavior. Instead of being reactive to daily news or stock price movements, they focus on the underlying health of the investments they've chosen. This patience and discipline help them avoid emotional decision-making and resist the urge to follow the herd during market bubbles or sell-offs.

Financial media and social media platforms can often amplify herd behavior by sensationalizing market moves and creating a sense of urgency. Constant exposure to market predictions, headlines about record highs or lows, and commentary from pundits can stir up emotions like fear or FOMO. This media-driven noise often encourages short-term thinking and increases the likelihood of making decisions based on what others are doing.

By limiting exposure to financial media and relying more on well-researched, longer-term data, investors can stay grounded. This helps to avoid impulsive actions and decisions driven by crowd sentiment rather than solid analysis. It's important to filter out the noise and focus on what matters most: long-term investment goals and personal financial plans.

A contrarian approach to investing involves doing the opposite of what the majority is doing. Contrarian investors recognize that markets are often driven by emotional reactions, leading to overvaluations or undervaluations. By deliberately seeking opportunities where others are fearful or overly exuberant, contrarians can often find value that the herd overlooks.

Famous investors like Warren Buffett have long advocated for this mindset, as evidenced by his well-known advice: "Be fearful when others are greedy, and be greedy when others are fearful." Contrarian investing requires discipline and patience, as it may take time for markets to correct and recognize the true value of underappreciated assets. However, it can be a highly effective way to avoid the perils of herd mentality.

Another strategy for resisting herd mentality is to adopt a systematic investment strategy, such as dollar-cost averaging (DCA). DCA involves investing a fixed amount of money into the market at regular intervals, regardless of price fluctuations. This strategy eliminates the emotional decision-making that often leads to buying high (due to FOMO) and selling low (due to panic).

By consistently investing, regardless of market conditions, investors can smooth out the effects of volatility over time. DCA also helps avoid the temptation to time the market, which is notoriously difficult and often driven by herd behavior. This disciplined approach ensures that investors stay invested during both market peaks and troughs, benefiting from long-term market growth.

Herd mentality in the stock market is a powerful

psychological force, deeply rooted in human nature and driven by a combination of social proof, FOMO, and cognitive biases. While following the crowd may offer short-term comfort, it often leads to irrational investment decisions, the inflation of market bubbles, and the devastation of market crashes.

To avoid falling into the trap of herd behavior, investors must develop strategies that emphasize independent research, long-term thinking, diversification, and disciplined decision-making. By doing so, they can navigate the ups and downs of the stock market with greater confidence and resilience, avoiding the costly mistakes that often come from following the crowd.

As technology and social media continue to shape the future of investing, the challenge of resisting herd mentality may become even more pronounced. However, by understanding the psychological drivers behind herd behavior and employing strategies to counteract it, investors can make more informed, rational decisions that will ultimately lead to greater financial success in the long run.

OVERCONFIDENCE AND THE ILLUSION OF CONTROL

The stock market has long been an arena for individuals and institutions to invest their money with the expectation of earning a return. However, the complexities of market dynamics and human psychology frequently lead investors to overestimate their ability to predict future market movements. This tendency can be attributed to a combination of cognitive biases, behavioral finance concepts, and the inherent unpredictability of market forces. Understanding these factors is crucial for investors looking to make informed decisions and avoid the pitfalls associated with overconfidence.

One of the most significant contributors to the overestimation of predictive ability in stock market investors is overconfidence bias. This psychological phenomenon occurs when individuals believe they possess more knowledge or skills than they actually do. In the context of investing, overconfident investors might think they can accurately predict market movements based on past performance or their analytical skills.

Investors often exhibit an illusion of control, believing

they can influence or predict random events. This bias leads them to think that their analysis and decisions will guarantee favorable outcomes. For instance, when investors conduct extensive research or use sophisticated tools to analyze stocks, they may feel a heightened sense of control over their investments. This false sense of mastery can lead them to disregard the role of chance in market movements.

Hindsight bias is another cognitive error that affects investors. After a market event occurs, investors tend to believe that they could have predicted the outcome all along. This retrospective insight can create an inflated sense of confidence in future predictions. For example, if an investor correctly predicts a market downturn after analyzing certain indicators, they may assume that similar indicators will yield accurate predictions in the future, overlooking the unpredictability of market conditions.

Emotions play a significant role in investment decisions, often clouding judgment and leading to overconfidence. Emotional investing can stem from various feelings, such as fear, greed, and excitement, which can skew rational analysis.

In the age of information, investors have access to a plethora of data, analyses, and news related to the stock market. While this information can be beneficial, it often leads to confusion and misinterpretation.

The vast amount of information available can overwhelm investors, making it challenging to discern relevant signals from noise. Investors may become overconfident in their ability to sift through data and identify meaningful patterns, leading them to make predictions based on flawed analyses or superficial observations. For example, an investor might rely on a single positive earnings report without considering broader market trends or macroeconomic factors.

Investors often fall prey to confirmation bias, which is the tendency to seek out information that supports their preconceived notions while ignoring contradictory evidence. This selective filtering of information can lead to a skewed understanding of market conditions and an overestimation of predictive abilities. For instance, an investor who believes a particular stock is undervalued may only focus on positive news related to that stock while disregarding negative developments that could affect its performance.

The stock market is inherently complex and influenced by various factors, including economic indicators, geopolitical events, and investor sentiment. This complexity makes it nearly impossible for any individual to predict market movements with consistent accuracy.

Market behavior is characterized by non-linear dynamics, where small changes in one area can lead to significant fluctuations elsewhere. This interconnectedness complicates prediction efforts, as investors may fail to recognize the broader implications of specific events. For example, a change in interest rates may not only affect bond markets but also impact consumer spending and corporate earnings, creating a ripple effect throughout the economy that is difficult to forecast.

Investors often underestimate the role of randomness in market movements. Events that are highly improbable yet impactful can dramatically shift market dynamics and render previous predictions obsolete. The unpredictability of such events emphasizes the limits of human foresight in financial markets.

Investor sentiment plays a crucial role in market movements, often leading to irrational behaviors and collective decision-making that can skew market predictions.

Investors frequently exhibit herd behavior, where they mimic the actions of others instead of relying on their analysis. This behavior can amplify market trends, creating bubbles and crashes that may seem predictable in hindsight. For instance, during a market rally, investors may feel compelled to join the frenzy, overestimating their ability to identify the top before a correction occurs.

The cyclical nature of fear and greed can further complicate investors' perceptions of market predictability. During bullish markets, greed can drive overconfidence, leading investors to believe they can maintain their winning streak. Conversely, during bearish markets, fear can trigger panic selling, causing investors to underestimate their capacity to recover or hold their positions for the long term.

The tendency to overestimate predictive ability can have severe consequences for investors, often leading to significant financial losses and emotional distress.

Overconfident investors are more likely to engage in riskier strategies, such as concentrated positions in a few stocks or speculative trades. This increased risk exposure can result in substantial losses, especially during market downturns when their predictions fail to materialize. Investors may find themselves trapped in losing positions, struggling to maintain their conviction in their earlier analyses.

The emotional toll of overestimating predictive ability can lead to stress and anxiety, impacting not only investment performance but also overall well-being. Investors may experience regret, frustration, or even anger when faced with losses, further clouding their judgment and decision-making processes.

To counteract the tendency to overestimate predictive abilities, investors can adopt several strategies aimed at promoting rational decision-making and reducing emotional bias.

Increasing financial literacy and understanding of market dynamics can help investors make more informed decisions. By recognizing the limitations of their predictive abilities and the role of psychological biases, investors can approach the market with greater humility and caution.

Implementing diversification strategies can help mitigate risks associated with overconfidence. By spreading investments across various asset classes, sectors, and geographic regions, investors can reduce the impact of individual stock fluctuations and minimize the potential for significant losses.

Focusing on long-term investment goals rather than short-term market predictions can promote a more disciplined investment approach. Investors should prioritize fundamental analysis and value investing over speculative trades driven by market sentiment or trends.

Working with financial advisors or investment professionals can provide valuable insights and help investors navigate the complexities of the market. Professional guidance can also assist in developing personalized investment strategies that account for individual risk tolerance and financial goals.

The stock market is a dynamic and unpredictable environment, making it essential for investors to recognize the limitations of their predictive abilities. Overconfidence, psychological biases, emotional factors, and the complexity of market dynamics all contribute to a widespread tendency among investors to overestimate their ability to predict future market movements. By fostering awareness of these influences and adopting prudent investment strategies, investors can make more informed decisions and better navigate the challenges of the stock market.

In the end, successful investing is not about predicting every market movement but rather about understanding the risks, staying disciplined, and maintaining a long-term perspective.

LOSS AVERSION: WHY PAIN HURTS MORE THAN GAIN

One of the most critical psychological concepts that impacts investor behavior is loss aversion. Rooted in behavioral economics, loss aversion describes the tendency of individuals to prefer avoiding losses over acquiring equivalent gains. This phenomenon has profound implications for stock market behavior, influencing investment decisions, risk tolerance, and overall market dynamics. Understanding loss aversion and its effects on stock market psychology is essential for both individual investors and market analysts.

Loss aversion was first introduced by psychologists Daniel Kahneman and Amos Tversky in their groundbreaking work on prospect theory. According to their findings, the pain of losing is psychologically more potent than the pleasure of an equivalent gain. In other words, the emotional impact of a loss is greater than that of a gain of the same magnitude. Kahneman and Tversky's research revealed that people tend to weigh losses more heavily than gains, leading to a skewed perception of risk and reward.

At its core, loss aversion is tied to emotional responses.

When individuals experience a loss, they often feel regret, disappointment, and anxiety, which can lead to irrational decision-making. Conversely, the feeling of gain is less intense, resulting in a less significant emotional response. This disparity can influence how investors react in various market conditions, especially during downturns or volatile periods.

Numerous studies support the concept of loss aversion. For example, research has shown that investors are more likely to hold onto losing stocks to avoid realizing a loss, a phenomenon known as the disposition effect. This behavior contradicts the rational investor model, which suggests that one should sell underperforming assets to reallocate capital to more promising investments. Instead, loss-averse investors often cling to losing stocks in hopes of a rebound, potentially leading to further losses.

The impact of loss aversion on stock market behavior manifests in various ways. It influences investor sentiment, trading patterns, and overall market dynamics.

During market downturns, loss aversion can lead to panic selling. When investors see their portfolios decline in value, the emotional weight of those losses often prompts irrational responses. This behavior can result in a rapid sell-off, exacerbating market declines as more investors react to the fear of further losses. The emotional response can overshadow rational analysis, leading to suboptimal decision-making.

Loss aversion is closely linked to herd behavior, where investors follow the actions of others rather than relying on their analysis. During periods of market uncertainty, such as significant drops or economic downturns, fear can spread quickly among investors. As individuals witness others selling off their stocks, they may feel compelled to do the same, creating a self-reinforcing cycle that further drives down stock prices. This behavior can lead to market inefficiencies, as stocks may become undervalued due to collective panic rather than fundamental analysis.

One of the most notable phenomena related to loss aversion in the stock market is the disposition effect. This refers to the tendency for investors to sell winning stocks while holding onto losing stocks longer than rational analysis would suggest.

Investors often develop emotional attachments to their investments, especially those that have performed well. Selling a winning stock can feel like a personal loss, leading to reluctance in taking profits. Selling a losing stock can be viewed as admitting a mistake. Investors may hold onto losing positions to avoid the psychological discomfort associated with realizing a loss. Loss-averse investors often hold onto underperforming stocks, hoping for a turnaround. This belief can cloud judgment and lead to further losses.

The disposition effect can adversely affect portfolio performance. By failing to cut losses and reallocating funds to more promising investments, investors may miss opportunities for better returns. Research has shown that investors who exhibit strong disposition effects tend to have lower overall returns compared to those who act more rationally.

Loss aversion interacts with several cognitive biases that further complicate stock market decision-making.

Anchoring bias occurs when investors rely too heavily on the initial price of an asset as a reference point. For example, if an investor buys a stock at $50 and the price drops to $30, they may anchor their perception of the stock's value to the original purchase price. This can lead to loss aversion as the investor fixates on the perceived loss rather than evaluating the stock's current fundamentals. The reluctance to sell at a loss may prevent them from making more informed investment decisions.

Confirmation bias refers to the tendency to seek

information that supports existing beliefs while ignoring contradictory evidence. Loss-averse investors may selectively focus on news or data that reinforces their hope for a recovery in a losing stock, disregarding negative information that suggests otherwise. This bias can hinder objective analysis and prolong holding onto underperforming investments.

The way information is presented can significantly impact decision-making. For instance, if a financial advisor frames an investment opportunity as having a potential loss of $100 versus a gain of $100, the emphasis on potential loss can trigger a stronger emotional reaction. This framing effect can lead to a risk-averse attitude, influencing investors to avoid opportunities that may have favorable long-term outcomes.

Understanding loss aversion is crucial for developing effective investment strategies. By recognizing the emotional biases at play, investors can create a more disciplined approach to managing their portfolios.

Establishing clear investment goals and sticking to them can help mitigate the emotional impact of loss aversion. By focusing on long-term objectives rather than short-term fluctuations, investors can avoid making impulsive decisions driven by fear.

Using stop-loss orders can help investors manage risk and limit losses. By predefining exit points, investors can take emotion out of the equation and avoid the psychological distress associated with holding onto losing positions.

Diversifying investments across various asset classes can reduce the impact of individual stock fluctuations. A well-diversified portfolio can help buffer against losses in any single investment, lessening the emotional impact of loss aversion.

Working with financial advisors can provide an objective perspective, helping investors navigate the emotional aspects of investing. Advisors can assist in developing rational investment strategies that account for loss aversion and cognitive biases.

Loss aversion is a cornerstone of behavioral finance, a field that combines psychology and economics to explain investor behavior. By understanding the psychological factors influencing decision-making, behavioral finance provides valuable insights into market dynamics.

Loss aversion contributes to several market anomalies, such as the equity premium puzzle and the January effect. The equity premium puzzle refers to the observation that stocks have historically outperformed bonds by a significant margin, despite the higher risks involved. Loss aversion may explain why investors demand a higher return on equities to compensate for the psychological discomfort of potential losses.

The January effect, a phenomenon where stock prices tend to rise in January, may also be linked to loss aversion. Investors often sell stocks at the end of the year to realize losses for tax purposes, leading to a temporary dip in prices. In January, as new capital flows into the market and investors re-enter, prices may rebound, driven by the psychological effects of loss aversion.

Understanding loss aversion can inform behavioral investment strategies. By acknowledging the emotional biases that influence decision-making, investors can develop strategies that align with their psychological tendencies. For instance, implementing a systematic investment plan, such as dollar-cost averaging, can help mitigate the impact of loss aversion by promoting consistent contributions regardless of market conditions.

Loss aversion is a powerful psychological force that significantly influences stock market behavior. Understanding this phenomenon is crucial for investors seeking to navigate the complexities of the market. By recognizing the emotional impact of losses, investors can develop strategies to mitigate the effects of loss aversion, enhance decision-making, and improve overall portfolio performance.

The interplay between loss aversion and stock market psychology highlights the need for a disciplined approach to investing. By combining behavioral insights with rational investment strategies, investors can better manage their emotions and make informed decisions. Recognizing the role of psychological biases in financial markets is essential for avoiding common pitfalls associated with loss aversion.

CONFIRMATION BIAS: SEEING WHAT YOU WANT TO SEE

Confirmation bias is a well-documented cognitive phenomenon that affects decision-making across various domains, including finance and investing. In the context of the stock market, confirmation bias can lead investors to seek out information that aligns with their existing beliefs while disregarding evidence that contradicts those beliefs. This tendency can have profound implications for investment strategies, market dynamics, and overall economic stability. Understanding confirmation bias is crucial for investors seeking to make rational decisions in a landscape often dominated by emotions and psychological factors.

At its core, confirmation bias is the tendency to search for, interpret, and remember information in a way that confirms one's preexisting beliefs or hypotheses. This cognitive bias leads individuals to prioritize information that supports their views while dismissing or undervaluing evidence that contradicts them. The phenomenon can manifest in various forms, including selective exposure to information, biased interpretation of ambiguous evidence, and distorted memory recall.

In the context of investing, confirmation bias can influence how investors analyze market trends, evaluate company performance, and interpret news events. For instance, if an investor believes that a particular stock will rise, they may only seek out positive news articles about that stock, overlooking negative reports or contrary analyses. This selective approach to information can create a feedback loop, reinforcing the investor's beliefs and leading to potentially irrational investment decisions.

Several psychological mechanisms contribute to the prevalence of confirmation bias in stock market behavior:

When individuals hold conflicting beliefs or encounter information that contradicts their views, they experience cognitive dissonance. To reduce this discomfort, they may ignore or rationalize contradictory information, further entrenching their existing beliefs. In investing, this can lead to an overreliance on favorable information and a dismissal of negative signals.

The social environment significantly impacts investor behavior. Investors often rely on their peers for insights and validation of their beliefs. In forums, social media, and investment clubs, individuals may reinforce each other's biases by sharing only information that aligns with their viewpoints, creating echo chambers that amplify confirmation bias.

Emotions play a vital role in financial decision-making. Fear, greed, and overconfidence can all exacerbate confirmation bias. For example, during bullish market conditions, investors may become overly optimistic and seek out information that validates their positive outlook, while during bearish conditions, fear can lead to a focus on negative information that confirms their pessimism.

Many investors exhibit overconfidence in their abilities to predict market movements or assess stock values. This overconfidence can lead to a reliance on personal beliefs and experiences rather than objective data. Consequently, investors may selectively focus on information that supports their confidence while dismissing contradictory evidence.

Understanding confirmation bias is crucial for investors seeking to navigate the complexities of the stock market effectively. Here are several implications of confirmation bias and strategies to mitigate its effects:

Investors should actively seek out diverse sources of information, including analyses that challenge their beliefs. Engaging with a variety of viewpoints can help counteract confirmation bias and lead to more informed decision-making.

Adopting a critical thinking approach is essential for investors. Instead of accepting information at face value, investors should evaluate the credibility of sources, scrutinize methodologies, and consider alternative explanations for market movements.

Recognizing the role of emotions in investment decisions can help investors maintain a more rational perspective. By acknowledging emotional influences and practicing mindfulness, investors can reduce the impact of confirmation bias on their decision-making processes.

Implementing feedback mechanisms, such as regularly reviewing investment performance and analyzing past decisions, can help investors identify patterns of confirmation bias. Reflecting on both successes and failures can lead to a more balanced understanding of market dynamics.

Establishing clear criteria for investment decisions can provide a framework for evaluating opportunities. By defining specific metrics for evaluating stocks or market conditions, investors can reduce the likelihood of succumbing to confirmation bias.

Engaging with other investors or seeking the input of financial professionals can provide valuable perspectives that challenge one's beliefs. Collaborative investing encourages open dialogue and diverse viewpoints, reducing the risk of confirmation bias.

Confirmation bias is a powerful force in stock market psychology, influencing the behavior and decision-making processes of investors. Understanding this cognitive bias is essential for investors looking to make rational, informed decisions in a complex and often irrational market environment. By recognizing the historical context, psychological mechanisms, and implications of confirmation bias, investors can develop strategies to mitigate its effects and navigate the stock market more effectively. In an era where information is abundant yet often misleading, cultivating a mindset that prioritizes critical thinking, emotional awareness, and diverse perspectives will be vital for successful investing.

THE ROLE OF FOMO

The stock market has always been a playground of emotions, and among the many psychological factors influencing investor behavior, few have garnered as much attention in recent years as FOMO, or the Fear of Missing Out. This phenomenon, characterized by the anxiety of potentially missing lucrative investment opportunities, has become increasingly prevalent, particularly with the rise of social media and online trading platforms. FOMO can lead to impulsive decision-making, market volatility, and a range of outcomes that can significantly impact investors' portfolios. Understanding the implications of FOMO in the stock market is essential for both novice and seasoned investors aiming to navigate this complex landscape effectively.

FOMO is a relatively modern term that gained traction in the early 2000s, primarily through the rise of social media. It encapsulates the anxiety individuals experience when they believe others are having rewarding experiences that they are not part of. While FOMO is often discussed in the context of social interactions—such as missing out on parties or events—it has also found a significant foothold in finance and investing. The stock market, with its constant updates and real-time trading, serves as a fertile ground for FOMO to flourish.

The concept of FOMO can be traced back to various psychological theories. The need for social connection, as described in Maslow's hierarchy of needs, plays a crucial role in FOMO. Additionally, the scarcity principle, which suggests that individuals place higher value on opportunities that appear limited, contributes to this phenomenon. In investing, the perception of a "hot" stock or market trend can trigger FOMO, leading investors to act out of fear rather than rational analysis.

FOMO can have profound psychological effects on investors, often leading to irrational decision-making. Some of the key psychological aspects of FOMO in the stock market include:

Impulsiveness: FOMO can drive investors to make hasty decisions without adequate research or analysis. This impulsiveness can result in buying high during market euphoria or selling low during panic.

Overtrading: Investors driven by FOMO may engage in excessive trading, constantly buying and selling stocks in an attempt to capitalize on fleeting opportunities. This behavior can lead to increased transaction costs and potential tax implications.

Emotional Distress: The anxiety associated with FOMO can create emotional distress for investors. The fear of making the wrong choice or missing out on potential gains can lead to stress and second-guessing, ultimately impacting decision-making.

Confirmation Bias: FOMO can exacerbate confirmation bias, where investors seek out information that supports their fear of missing out while ignoring evidence that contradicts their beliefs. This selective focus can reinforce irrational investment strategies.

FOMO can significantly influence investment decisions, leading to both short-term and long-term consequences. Understanding these impacts can help investors navigate the complexities of the stock market more effectively.

Many investors, particularly retail traders, are drawn into the stock market by the prospect of quick profits. FOMO can drive short-term trading strategies, characterized by rapid buying and selling based on market trends and social media chatter. While this approach can yield immediate gains, it often comes with significant risks.

Short-term trading driven by FOMO can contribute to increased market volatility. Rapid buying and selling can lead to exaggerated price movements, creating a rollercoaster effect that can be detrimental to both individual investors and the broader market.

Short-term traders influenced by FOMO may make decisions based on emotions rather than sound analysis. This can result in missed opportunities for long-term gains and increased exposure to losses.

FOMO can also impact long-term investment strategies, leading investors to deviate from their original plans. For instance:

Investors may feel compelled to chase high-performing stocks, abandoning their carefully constructed portfolios. This behavior can lead to a lack of diversification and increased risk.

FOMO can drive investors to attempt to time the market, selling off underperforming assets in a panic or buying into popular stocks at inflated prices. This strategy is notoriously difficult to execute successfully and often leads to poor outcomes.

Investors influenced by FOMO may neglect thorough research and analysis, relying instead on trends and social media buzz. This lack of due diligence can result in uninformed investment decisions and missed opportunities for meaningful growth.

FOMO does not only impact individual investors; it can also have broader economic implications. Understanding these effects can provide context for the behavior observed in financial markets.

When FOMO drives a significant number of investors to

buy or sell stocks en masse, it can lead to increased market volatility. This volatility can be exacerbated by:

When investors follow the crowd, it can create rapid price changes that are not necessarily aligned with the underlying fundamentals of the stocks involved.

In a highly interconnected financial ecosystem, algorithmic trading can amplify FOMO-driven behavior, leading to rapid price movements and potential market disruptions.

FOMO is a powerful psychological phenomenon that significantly impacts investor behavior in the stock market. Amplified by social media and instant access to information, FOMO can lead to impulsive decisions, increased market volatility, and detrimental long-term outcomes. Understanding the origins and implications of FOMO is crucial for investors seeking to navigate the complexities of the stock market effectively.

By developing a solid investment plan, conducting thorough research, limiting social media exposure, practicing mindfulness, and embracing a long-term perspective, investors can mitigate the negative effects of FOMO. Additionally, recognizing the broader economic implications of FOMO-driven behavior can inform discussions around regulation and responsible investing practices.

Ultimately, overcoming FOMO requires a commitment to rational decision-making and an awareness of the emotional influences at play in the investment landscape. By fostering a mindset grounded in analysis rather than anxiety, investors can position themselves for more sustainable success in the dynamic world of the stock market.

RISK PERCEPTION

Risk perception is a critical factor influencing investment decisions in the stock market. Understanding how individuals and institutions perceive risk can shed light on market behaviors, investment strategies, and overall market dynamics. This essay explores the multifaceted relationship between risk perception and the stock market, examining its implications for investors, market volatility, behavioral finance, and the role of external factors in shaping risk perceptions.

Risk perception refers to an individual's or a group's subjective judgment about the severity and likelihood of a risk. It is influenced by various factors, including personal experiences, cultural background, media portrayal, and cognitive biases. Unlike objective risk, which can be quantified and measured, risk perception is inherently subjective and can vary significantly among individuals.

In the context of the stock market, several types of risk can affect investor perception:

Market Risk: This refers to the risk of losses due to overall market fluctuations. Factors influencing market risk include economic indicators, political events, and global crises.

Credit Risk: This is the risk that a company will default on its debt obligations, affecting its stock price and, consequently, investors' portfolios.

Liquidity Risk: This involves the risk of not being able to sell an investment quickly without incurring significant losses.

Operational Risk: This is related to failures in internal processes, systems, or human errors within a company that could impact its financial performance and stock price.

Systematic and Unsystematic Risk: Systematic risk affects the entire market and cannot be diversified away (e.g., economic recessions), while unsystematic risk is specific to a particular company or industry and can be mitigated through diversification.

Understanding these risks is essential for investors as they navigate the complexities of the stock market.

Behavioral finance provides insight into how cognitive biases and emotional responses affect risk perception and decision-making in the stock market. Some key concepts include:

Many investors overestimate their ability to predict market movements, leading to excessive trading and increased risk exposure.

Investors tend to feel the pain of losses more acutely than the pleasure of gains, which can lead to irrational decision-making, such as holding onto losing stocks for too long.

Investors often follow the crowd, leading to market bubbles and crashes. When individuals perceive risk through the lens of collective sentiment, they may ignore their own analysis.

Investors may rely too heavily on initial information or specific price points when making decisions, which can skew their perception of risk.

Understanding these biases is crucial for investors seeking to manage their risk perception effectively.

Risk perception directly influences investment decisions. An investor's assessment of risk can dictate their asset allocation, trading strategies, and overall investment approach.

Here are some ways in which risk perception affects investment decisions:

Investors have different levels of risk tolerance, which can be influenced by their experiences, age, financial situation, and psychological factors. Those with a higher risk tolerance may be more willing to invest in volatile stocks or sectors, while risk-averse investors may prefer more stable, income-generating investments.

Investors often diversify their portfolios based on their perception of risk. A risk-averse investor may allocate a larger portion of their portfolio to bonds or other fixed-income securities, while a more risk-tolerant investor may invest heavily in equities, especially in high-growth sectors.

Risk perception can lead to market timing strategies, where investors attempt to buy low and sell high based on their interpretation of market conditions. However, accurately timing the market is notoriously challenging and can lead to significant losses.

Investors' reactions to market events, such as economic downturns, geopolitical tensions, or company-specific news, are heavily influenced by their risk perception. Panic selling during market downturns often stems from heightened risk perception, leading to increased volatility.

Investors who perceive risk as a long-term concern may adopt a buy-and-hold strategy, focusing on fundamental analysis and the intrinsic value of stocks. Conversely, those with a short-term perspective may engage in speculative trading, reacting to market trends and news.

Market volatility is often a reflection of changing risk perceptions among investors. High volatility periods are usually characterized by increased uncertainty and fear, which can lead to significant fluctuations in stock prices. The relationship between risk perception and market volatility can be understood through several lenses:

The stock market is often influenced by the dual forces of fear and greed. When investors perceive heightened risk, fear can lead to panic selling, exacerbating market downturns. Conversely, periods of low perceived risk can result in over-exuberance and rising prices.

Market indicators, such as the VIX (Volatility Index), measure market expectations of future volatility. A rising VIX often correlates with increased risk perception, signaling that investors are anticipating turbulent times ahead.

Key economic indicators, such as unemployment rates, inflation, and GDP growth, can shift risk perceptions among investors. Negative economic news can heighten perceived risk, leading to increased market volatility.

Political instability, trade tensions, and global conflicts can dramatically alter investors' risk perceptions. Uncertainty surrounding geopolitical events often leads to heightened volatility as investors react to potential risks.

The flow of information plays a crucial role in shaping risk perception in the stock market. In the digital age, information spreads rapidly, impacting investor sentiment and decision-making. Here are some key aspects to consider:

News coverage of market events, economic indicators, and corporate earnings can significantly impact risk perception. Sensationalized reporting can create undue panic or optimism, influencing investor behavior.

Social Media: Platforms like Twitter and Reddit have become powerful tools for disseminating information and shaping investor sentiment. Viral trends can lead to sudden shifts in risk perception, often resulting in rapid buying or selling.

Analysts' ratings and recommendations can influence investors' perceptions of risk. Positive ratings may reduce perceived risk, while negative reports can heighten caution.

Companies that communicate openly and transparently with investors can help mitigate risk perception. Clear guidance on financial performance and strategy can foster investor confidence, while uncertainty can heighten perceived risk.

The perception of risk can differ significantly between institutional and retail investors. Institutional investors, such as pension funds and hedge funds, often have access to extensive research and resources that enable them to assess risk more objectively. In contrast, retail investors may rely more on intuition, media reports, and emotional responses.

Institutional investors often employ sophisticated risk management strategies, using derivatives and hedging techniques to mitigate risk. Retail investors, on the other hand, may lack the knowledge or resources to implement similar strategies.

Risk Tolerance: Institutional investors typically have a lower risk tolerance due to fiduciary responsibilities and regulatory constraints. Retail investors, however, may be more willing to take on risk in pursuit of higher returns.

Market Impact: Institutional investors tend to have a more significant influence on market movements due to their large trading volumes. Their risk assessments can shape market dynamics and affect retail investors' perceptions of risk.

Herd Behavior: Retail investors are more susceptible to herd behavior, often following trends and popular sentiments without thorough analysis. Institutional investors, while also subject to market sentiment, are typically more disciplined in their decision-making.

Risk perception is a vital aspect of the stock market, influencing investment decisions, market volatility, and overall market dynamics. Understanding the psychological and behavioral factors that shape risk perception can help investors navigate the complexities of the stock market more effectively. As markets continue to evolve in response to global events, technological advancements, and changing investor behaviors, recognizing the role of risk perception will be essential for making informed investment decisions and managing portfolio risks.

By fostering a deeper understanding of risk perception and its implications, investors can better position themselves for success in the ever-changing landscape of the stock market.

ANCHORING: THE DANGER OF FIRST IMPRESSIONS

The stock market operates in an environment characterized by uncertainty and volatility, where a myriad of factors can influence the price of securities. Among these factors, initial information plays a pivotal role in shaping investors' perceptions and decisions. This paper examines how initial information, whether positive or negative, can impact future decisions made by investors and analysts, leading to potential biases, herd behavior, and the long-term consequences for market efficiency.

Initial information refers to the first pieces of data or news that an investor encounters regarding a particular stock or the market as a whole. This could include:

Earnings Reports: Quarterly results that show a company's profitability.

Economic Indicators: Reports on unemployment rates, inflation, and GDP growth.

Market Sentiment: General feelings of investors based on news and media coverage.

Analyst Recommendations: Initial ratings and price targets set by financial analysts.

The impact of initial information can be understood through psychological concepts like anchoring and confirmation bias. Anchoring occurs when individuals rely too heavily on the first piece of information they receive (the "anchor") when making subsequent judgments. Confirmation bias leads investors to seek out information that supports their initial beliefs while disregarding contradictory data.

Investors may fixate on the initial price of a stock or the first earnings report they see, leading them to make decisions based on this anchor rather than considering new, potentially conflicting information. When initial information generates widespread reactions among investors, it can create a bandwagon effect, where individuals follow the crowd, often disregarding their independent analysis. Initial positive information can lead to overconfidence in investment strategies. Investors may believe they have superior knowledge and neglect the potential for loss.

In many cases, the information available to investors is not equal. Those with access to privileged or early information (e.g., insider trading) can make more informed decisions, further skewing market efficiency. The influence of initial information can be exacerbated when institutional investors or analysts dominate the conversation, as their interpretations often shape public perception.

The initial reaction to information often results in immediate price adjustments. For example, if a company reports unexpectedly high earnings, the stock price may surge as investors rush to buy shares. Conversely, negative news can lead to rapid sell-offs. These initial price changes can establish new reference points that guide future decisions.

While initial reactions are often short-lived, they can set the stage for long-term trends. If a stock experiences an initial surge due to positive news, subsequent investors may perceive it as a "hot" stock, leading to sustained buying pressure. Conversely, stocks that experience initial declines may face a prolonged period of underperformance as investors remain cautious.

The framing effect describes how the presentation of information can influence decision-making. For instance, if a company's earnings are reported as a percentage increase rather than a specific dollar amount, investors may perceive the performance more favorably, leading to different investment decisions.

Initial information can evoke strong emotional responses. Positive news may lead to excitement and greed, while negative news can trigger fear and panic. These emotions can cloud judgment and lead to impulsive decisions, often contrary to rational analysis.

According to the Efficient Market Hypothesis, all available information should be reflected in stock prices, making it impossible to achieve consistently higher returns. However, the influence of initial information challenges this theory, as biases and irrational behavior can lead to mispriced securities. Investors reacting disproportionately to initial news can create opportunities for those willing to take a contrarian approach.

Understanding the influence of initial information encourages investors to approach the market with skepticism. Relying solely on initial impressions can lead to poor investment outcomes. Savvy investors often look for comprehensive analyses and long-term trends rather than reacting to immediate news.

Initial information significantly shapes investor decisions in the stock market. The psychological biases, emotional reactions, and cognitive processes triggered by this information can lead to both positive and negative outcomes. By recognizing the profound impact of initial news, investors can strive for more informed decision-making and avoid the pitfalls associated with irrational behavior.

Investors are often swayed by the first pieces of information they encounter, which can create anchors that guide their perceptions and decisions moving forward. This phenomenon is amplified by cognitive biases, such as anchoring and confirmation bias, which can lead to suboptimal decision-making and herd behavior.

Initial information can trigger immediate market reactions, resulting in significant price volatility. These initial responses can establish reference points that shape future investor behavior, leading to long-term trends based on initial sentiment rather than fundamental analysis.

The emotional responses triggered by initial news, whether excitement over positive earnings or fear stemming from negative reports, can cloud judgment and prompt impulsive decisions. This underscores the importance of critical analysis and a long-term perspective in investing, rather than knee-jerk reactions to market news.

Ultimately, while initial information serves as a crucial input in investment decision-making, it is essential for investors to remain vigilant, aware of the potential biases at play, and committed to a disciplined investment strategy. By recognizing the influence of initial information, investors can navigate the complexities of the stock market more effectively, leading to more rational decisions and improved investment outcomes.

RECENCY BIAS: LIVING IN THE NOW

In the complex world of investing, numerous psychological factors influence decision-making processes. Among these, recency bias stands out as a significant phenomenon that can skew investor perceptions and behaviors. Recency bias refers to the tendency for individuals to place greater importance on recent events or experiences compared to earlier ones, leading to distorted judgments and expectations. This paper delves into the nature of recency bias, its psychological underpinnings, its manifestations in the stock market, and its implications for investors.

Recency bias is a cognitive bias that occurs when individuals disproportionately weigh recent experiences more heavily than earlier ones. This can lead to an overemphasis on short-term trends while neglecting long-term data and patterns. In investing, this bias can result in a skewed perception of a stock's potential performance based on its most recent price movements or news.

The psychological underpinnings of recency bias are rooted in human cognition and memory. Several factors contribute to this bias:

Availability Heuristic: This mental shortcut relies on immediate examples that come to mind when evaluating a situation. If an investor recently witnessed a stock surge or decline, they may perceive this trend as more probable or important than historical data.

Loss Aversion: According to behavioral finance, investors feel the pain of losses more acutely than the pleasure of equivalent gains. Recent negative events can heighten this sensitivity, leading investors to act more conservatively after a downturn.

Recent events often evoke stronger emotional responses, which can cloud rational judgment. Fear from recent market volatility or excitement from positive earnings can lead investors to make impulsive decisions.

Recency bias significantly influences market sentiment, which is critical for stock price movements. When recent events —be they economic indicators, earnings reports, or geopolitical developments—dominate news cycles, they can shape collective investor attitudes and expectations.

If a company reports strong earnings, investors may extrapolate this performance into the future, resulting in aggressive buying. Conversely, poor earnings can lead to sell-offs, driven by a fear that the negative trend will continue.

Investors often follow recent trends, leading to herd behavior where many buy or sell simultaneously based on recent performance. This behavior can exacerbate price swings and create feedback loops that reinforce the bias.

Recency bias can distort the balance between short-term and long-term investment strategies. Investors influenced by recent events may prioritize short-term gains, neglecting the fundamentals that typically govern long-term stock performance.

After a period of strong performance, investors may feel compelled to chase returns, buying into stocks that have recently surged without adequate analysis of their underlying value.

Investors may ignore critical fundamental analysis in favor of recent price movements. For example, a stock may have a strong history of profitability, but a recent decline could lead investors to prematurely sell, missing out on potential recovery.

Recency bias can contribute to increased market volatility, as investors react strongly to recent news or events without fully considering the broader context. This behavior can lead to rapid price fluctuations and mispricing, creating opportunities for traders but also increasing risks for long-term investors.

Investors influenced by recency bias may make decisions that are not aligned with their long-term financial goals. This could involve frequent trading based on recent performance rather than a consistent investment strategy, leading to higher transaction costs and potential losses.

When many investors succumb to recency bias, the risk of market bubbles increases. Investors chasing recent high returns can drive prices beyond sustainable levels, creating an unsustainable market that is vulnerable to sudden corrections.

Developing a well-defined investment strategy that prioritizes long-term goals can help counteract the effects of recency bias. By focusing on fundamental analysis and diversified portfolios, investors can reduce their reliance on recent trends.

Adopting risk management strategies, such as setting stop-loss orders or diversifying across asset classes, can help mitigate the impact of recency bias on investment decisions.

Practicing emotional discipline is essential for countering recency bias. Investors should strive to recognize their emotional responses to market movements and commit to rational decision-making based on a consistent strategy.

Recency bias profoundly shapes investor expectations and actions in the stock market, often leading to distorted perceptions and impulsive decision-making. The tendency to overemphasize recent events can result in increased volatility, poor investment choices, and the risk of market bubbles.

By understanding the mechanisms behind recency bias and recognizing its manifestations, investors can take proactive steps to mitigate its influence. Establishing a long-term investment strategy, conducting regular portfolio reviews, seeking diverse perspectives, implementing risk management techniques, and maintaining emotional discipline are all effective strategies for counteracting recency bias.

Cultivating awareness of this cognitive bias empowers investors to make more informed, rational decisions that align with their financial goals, promoting a healthier investment approach in a complex and often unpredictable market environment.

MARKET EUPHORIA: THE PSYCHOLOGY OF BUBBLES

Bubbles have captivated economists, psychologists, and sociologists alike for centuries. They manifest in various forms, from economic and financial bubbles to social and cultural phenomena. Understanding the psychology behind bubbles provides insight into human behavior, decision-making, and the collective mindset that can lead to irrational exuberance or despair. This exploration will delve into the psychological underpinnings of bubbles, examining how emotions, cognitive biases, and social dynamics contribute to their formation and eventual collapse.

A bubble, in economic terms, refers to a situation where the prices of assets, such as stocks, real estate, or commodities, inflate beyond their intrinsic value, driven by exuberant speculation. Bubbles are often characterized by rapid price increases followed by sudden crashes. Historically, numerous examples illustrate the phenomenon, including the Tulip Mania of the 1630s in the Netherlands, the South Sea Bubble in the early 18th century, and the dot-com bubble of the late 1990s.

Each of these bubbles shares a common thread: an

initial spark of enthusiasm leads to widespread participation, culminating in unsustainable price growth. The aftermath is often a harsh reckoning as the bubble bursts, resulting in financial loss and psychological distress for many involved.

One of the key psychological factors contributing to bubble formation is herd behavior. Humans are social creatures, and the desire to conform to group behavior can significantly influence individual decision-making. When investors observe others profiting from rising asset prices, they may feel compelled to join in, driven by the fear of missing out (FOMO).

Herd behavior can be particularly pronounced in environments characterized by uncertainty, where individuals look to others for cues on how to act. This behavior can create a feedback loop: as more people buy into the bubble, prices rise, attracting even more participants. This phenomenon is well-documented in behavioral finance, where it's shown that individuals often prioritize group dynamics over rational analysis.

Overconfidence plays a significant role in bubble psychology. Many investors overestimate their ability to predict market movements, leading them to engage in risky behavior. This overconfidence is fueled by an optimism bias, where individuals believe that positive outcomes are more likely than negative ones. As asset prices rise, investors may become increasingly convinced that the upward trend will continue indefinitely.

This combination of overconfidence and optimism can blind individuals to the fundamental realities of the market. They may disregard warning signs or dismiss negative information, leading to an inflated sense of security. The result is a fragile market environment where prices are driven more by sentiment than by underlying value.

Anchoring is a cognitive bias where individuals rely heavily on the first piece of information they encounter when making decisions. In the context of bubbles, early adopters or those who invested at lower prices may anchor their expectations based on those initial investments. As prices rise, they may continue to reference their original purchase prices, believing that the asset's value will always return to or exceed those levels.

This reliance on reference points can perpetuate the bubble, as investors hold onto their assets despite rising risks. They may convince themselves that market corrections are temporary and that prices will rebound, delaying their response to changing market conditions.

Social proof, the psychological phenomenon where individuals look to others for validation of their actions, plays a crucial role in bubble dynamics. As more people invest in a particular asset, a sense of legitimacy builds around the investment. The social endorsement of an asset can create a bandwagon effect, where individuals feel compelled to participate to avoid being left out.

This phenomenon is exacerbated by the rise of social media and online forums, where discussions around investment opportunities can create a sense of community and shared purpose. In these environments, confirmation bias can flourish, as individuals seek out information that supports their beliefs while ignoring dissenting viewpoints.

Cultural narratives and shared beliefs also shape bubble psychology. In times of economic prosperity, narratives emphasizing growth and opportunity can foster an environment ripe for bubble formation. The collective identity of investors may shift towards a mindset of abundance, where risk is downplayed, and potential rewards are emphasized.

This cultural context can further reinforce herd behavior, as individuals align their identities with the prevailing investment trends. The narrative surrounding a bubble often involves stories of ordinary people achieving extraordinary wealth, reinforcing the notion that anyone can succeed in the market.

When a bubble bursts, the psychological impact can be profound. Cognitive dissonance, the mental discomfort experienced when holding contradictory beliefs, often emerges. Investors who were previously confident in their decisions may struggle to reconcile their beliefs with the harsh reality of financial loss. This dissonance can lead to a range of emotional responses, from anger and denial to anxiety and depression.

Individuals may seek to rationalize their decisions or blame external factors for their losses, distancing themselves from their prior actions. This response can hinder learning from the experience, as individuals may not fully confront the psychological biases that contributed to their participation in the bubble.

The aftermath of a bubble burst often triggers intense fear and loss aversion, where individuals prioritize avoiding losses over acquiring gains. This emotional response can lead to a heightened sense of caution and reluctance to invest in future opportunities. The psychological scars left by the experience can result in a more risk-averse mindset, affecting decision-making for years to come.

Loss aversion can also influence market dynamics following a bubble burst. As investors panic and sell off assets to minimize losses, they can exacerbate downward price trends, creating a self-fulfilling prophecy where fear drives further declines.

Regret is another significant psychological factor that emerges after a bubble burst. Investors may experience regret for not selling at the peak or for succumbing to peer pressure. This regret can lead to a reluctance to re-enter the market, as individuals may fear making similar mistakes in the future.

The emotional toll of regret can foster a sense of mistrust

towards market dynamics and investment opportunities. Individuals may become more skeptical and less willing to engage in future investments, limiting their potential for financial growth.

Understanding the psychology of bubbles can inform strategies for mitigating their risks. Education and awareness are crucial in helping individuals recognize the psychological biases that can influence decision-making. By fostering a culture of critical thinking and skepticism, investors can better evaluate opportunities and resist the allure of speculative behavior.

Promoting financial literacy can empower individuals to make informed decisions based on sound fundamentals rather than emotional impulses. Encouraging open discussions about the risks and potential pitfalls of investing can help create a more balanced perspective, reducing the likelihood of herd behavior and irrational exuberance.

Regulatory frameworks can also play a role in mitigating bubble dynamics. Policymakers can implement measures to ensure transparency and accountability within financial markets, discouraging predatory lending practices and fostering a healthier investment environment. By addressing the psychological factors that contribute to bubbles, it's possible to create a more stable economic landscape.

The psychology of bubbles is a multifaceted phenomenon that intertwines cognitive biases, social influences, and emotional dynamics, profoundly affecting individual and collective decision-making. As evidenced by historical examples such as the dot-com and housing bubbles, the allure of speculative investment often blinds participants to underlying realities, fostering a climate of overconfidence and herd behavior. These psychological factors create a feedback loop that can propel asset prices to unsustainable heights, ultimately culminating in a dramatic collapse.

Understanding the psychological mechanisms at play,

such as loss aversion, cognitive dissonance, and the impact of cultural narratives can help individuals and markets better navigate the risks associated with bubbles. By promoting financial literacy, encouraging critical thinking, and fostering a culture of skepticism, we can mitigate the psychological traps that lead to irrational exuberance and devastating financial repercussions.

In recognizing the role of human psychology in the formation and bursting of bubbles, we gain valuable insights into our decision-making processes and the need for vigilance in our investment behaviors. Ultimately, a deeper understanding of these dynamics not only enriches our comprehension of market phenomena but also empowers us to make more informed and rational choices, safeguarding against the pitfalls of speculative excess.

THE GAMBLER'S FALLACY: BETTING ON LUCK

The gambler's fallacy, often encapsulated in the saying "a win is due," refers to the misconception that past independent events affect the probabilities of future outcomes in random situations. Commonly observed in gambling contexts, this cognitive bias can lead individuals to make irrational decisions based on the mistaken belief that a specific outcome is "due" after a series of different results. The fallacy extends beyond the gambling table, influencing various aspects of life, including investment decisions, sports, and even everyday choices. This exploration delves into the mechanisms, implications, and broader context of the gambler's fallacy, illuminating its psychological roots and societal impact.

The gambler's fallacy, also known as the Monte Carlo fallacy or the fallacy of the maturity of chances, arises from a fundamental misunderstanding of probability. It occurs when individuals believe that the outcomes of random events can somehow influence one another, leading to erroneous predictions about future events.

Historically, the term gained traction following the

infamous Monte Carlo Casino incident in 1913, when a roulette wheel landed on black 26 times in a row. Observers, convinced that a red outcome was overdue, placed large bets on red, resulting in substantial losses. This incident vividly illustrated how psychological biases can lead to misinformed betting behaviors, setting the stage for further exploration into the cognitive processes behind the fallacy.

At the core of the gambler's fallacy is a misunderstanding of the independence of random events. In a fair game of chance, such as roulette or flipping a coin, each outcome is statistically independent. This means that previous outcomes have no bearing on the probability of future results. However, individuals often perceive patterns where none exist, leading them to believe that certain outcomes are "due" after a series of different results.

For example, if a coin has landed on heads five times in a row, a person might assume that tails is more likely on the next flip. In reality, the probability remains unchanged at 50% for each flip. This cognitive bias stems from the human tendency to seek patterns and assign meaning to randomness, a phenomenon known as apophenia.

The gambler's fallacy is often contrasted with the "hot hand" fallacy, where individuals believe that a person who has experienced success in the past is more likely to continue experiencing success in the future. While the gambler's fallacy focuses on the belief that a negative outcome is overdue, the hot hand fallacy embodies the belief in a streak of good fortune.

Both fallacies illustrate the human propensity to perceive patterns and sequences in random events. The underlying cognitive mechanisms involve the same psychological processes, including confirmation bias and the tendency to attribute success or failure to specific factors rather than chance.

Cognitive dissonance can also play a role in reinforcing

the gambler's fallacy. When individuals experience a series of losses, they may struggle to reconcile their beliefs about luck or fate with the reality of their situation. To resolve this discomfort, they may convince themselves that a win is imminent, leading to increased risk-taking behaviors.

This dissonance can perpetuate a cycle of irrational decision-making, as individuals double down on their beliefs and continue to gamble in the hope of validating their expectations. The emotional investment in the belief that a win is "due" can lead to significant financial losses, reinforcing the fallacy.

The gambler's fallacy can have serious financial implications for individuals. Those who fall prey to this cognitive bias may find themselves engaging in reckless gambling behaviors, leading to significant losses. The belief that a win is overdue can prompt individuals to place larger bets or increase their frequency of play, ultimately exacerbating their financial troubles.

This pattern is particularly concerning in environments such as casinos, where the odds are inherently stacked against the player. The allure of potential payouts combined with the gambler's fallacy can create a dangerous cycle, as individuals chase losses in the hopes of a "big win."

The gambler's fallacy extends beyond individual behavior, influencing broader societal trends. In financial markets, for example, investors may exhibit similar biases when making decisions about stocks or commodities. The belief that a stock is "due" for a rebound after a series of losses can lead to poor investment choices and increased market volatility.

The gambler's fallacy can be observed in other domains, such as sports betting and lottery participation. Fans may believe that their favorite team is more likely to win after a losing streak or that specific lottery numbers are "due" to appear, perpetuating irrational betting behaviors.

Numerous psychological experiments have demonstrated the prevalence of the gambler's fallacy. One classic study involved participants observing a series of coin tosses. When presented with sequences of heads and tails, many participants exhibited the gambler's fallacy by predicting that the opposite outcome was due, despite the independence of each flip.

This experiment highlights the inherent cognitive biases that influence decision-making in random contexts. Participants' reliance on perceived patterns led them to make erroneous predictions, illustrating how deeply ingrained the gambler's fallacy can be in human thought processes.

Research has also examined the gambler's fallacy in the context of lottery participation. Studies have shown that individuals who have recently lost in lottery games are more likely to believe that they are due for a win in future draws. This belief can lead to increased spending on lottery tickets, despite the odds remaining constant.

These findings underscore the psychological mechanisms at play, as participants seek to rationalize their past losses and reinforce their belief in the possibility of future success.

Understanding the gambler's fallacy is essential for mitigating its effects and promoting more rational decision-making. Several strategies can help individuals recognize and counteract this cognitive bias.

Increasing awareness of the gambler's fallacy and its psychological underpinnings is a crucial step in combating its influence. Educational initiatives can inform individuals about the nature of probability, randomness, and the independence of events. By understanding the fallacy, individuals can better recognize when they are falling prey to irrational beliefs.

Implementing structured decision-making frameworks can also help individuals avoid the pitfalls of the gambler's fallacy. By focusing on objective data, statistical analysis, and risk assessment, individuals can make more informed choices that are less influenced by cognitive biases.

In gambling scenarios, players can establish strict budgets and adhere to predetermined betting strategies. By relying on rational decision-making processes, individuals can mitigate the emotional influences that contribute to the gambler's fallacy.

Practicing mindfulness and reflection can enhance individuals' awareness of their thought patterns and decision-making processes. By fostering a non-judgmental awareness of thoughts and feelings, individuals can create space for rational analysis and reduce the impact of cognitive biases.

Mindfulness techniques, such as meditation or journaling, can help individuals develop greater self-awareness and clarity in their decision-making. By recognizing when they are falling into the gambler's fallacy, individuals can consciously redirect their thoughts towards more rational perspectives.

The gambler's fallacy is part of a larger tapestry of human cognition related to chance and uncertainty. Understanding this context can provide valuable insights into how individuals navigate risk in various domains of life.

Human beings have a complex relationship with risk. While some individuals embrace risk as an opportunity for reward, others are more cautious and risk-averse. The gambler's fallacy illustrates how perceptions of risk can be distorted by cognitive biases, leading individuals to engage in behaviors that do not align with rational probability.

Research in behavioral economics highlights the importance of understanding how individuals perceive risk and uncertainty. By exploring the psychological factors that influence decision-making, we can gain insights into broader trends in gambling, investing, and other risk-related behaviors.

Emotions play a significant role in shaping decision-making processes, particularly in high-stakes situations. The gambler's fallacy is often fueled by emotional factors such as excitement, anxiety, and the desire for validation. Understanding the emotional undercurrents of decision-making can provide a more comprehensive view of how individuals navigate uncertainty.

The thrill of gambling can create a euphoric state that clouds judgment and leads to reckless behavior. Conversely, fear of loss can prompt individuals to make irrational decisions in an attempt to regain control. By recognizing the interplay between emotions and cognitive biases, individuals can cultivate greater emotional intelligence in their decision-making.

The gambler's fallacy serves as a poignant reminder of the complexities of human cognition and decision-making. Rooted in misunderstandings of probability and influenced by cognitive biases, this fallacy can lead individuals to make irrational choices that carry significant financial and emotional consequences.

By exploring the psychological mechanisms, societal implications, and strategies for mitigating its effects, we can foster a deeper understanding of the gambler's fallacy and its broader context within the landscape of chance and uncertainty. Through education, awareness, and mindful decision-making, individuals can break free from the grip of this cognitive bias and navigate the complexities of risk with greater clarity and rationality.

The gambler's fallacy underscores the importance of recognizing the limitations of our cognitive processes in the face of randomness. By cultivating a more nuanced understanding of chance, we can make informed decisions that align with reality rather than succumbing to the allure of mistaken beliefs.

THE SUNK COST FALLACY

The sunk cost fallacy is a cognitive bias that occurs when individuals continue an endeavor or investment due to previously invested resources (time, money, effort) rather than evaluating the current situation and future potential outcomes. This fallacy is particularly pronounced in the stock market, where investors often find themselves grappling with the emotional weight of their past decisions. By understanding the sunk cost fallacy, investors can make more rational decisions, minimizing losses and maximizing potential gains.

The concept of the sunk cost fallacy can be traced back to behavioral economics and psychology. It describes the tendency of individuals to stick with a decision based on the cumulative prior investment, despite new evidence suggesting that the current situation might not justify the continuation of that decision.

Several psychological mechanisms contribute to the sunk cost fallacy:

Loss Aversion: According to prospect theory, people prefer to avoid losses rather than acquiring equivalent gains. This aversion leads investors to hold onto losing stocks in hopes of recouping their losses rather than cutting their losses and reallocating their capital.

Commitment and Consistency: Humans have a strong desire to appear consistent in their decisions. Once individuals commit to an investment, they may feel compelled to justify that decision by continuing to invest, even when the situation has changed.

Emotional Investment: The emotional connection to past investments can cloud judgment. Investors often develop attachments to certain stocks, making it challenging to make objective decisions regarding their performance.

A common scenario illustrating the sunk cost fallacy involves an investor who buys shares of a company for $100 per share. Over time, the stock price drops to $50. Instead of selling and cutting losses, the investor may hold onto the shares, hoping that the price will return to its original value. This decision is based on the previous investment rather than the stock's current performance or future prospects.

Another example is when an investor has already invested significant capital in a poorly performing mutual fund. Even if analysis suggests that other funds could provide better returns, the investor may hesitate to switch, feeling that their past contributions should not be wasted.

In the stock market, the sunk cost fallacy manifests in various ways, influencing individual and institutional investors alike.

One of the most prevalent consequences of the sunk cost fallacy is the tendency to hold onto losing stocks. Investors often refuse to sell, believing that selling would validate their poor decision-making. This behavior can be detrimental, as it ties up capital that could be better utilized elsewhere.

Consider an investor who bought shares of a tech company at $120 each, only to see the stock plummet to $30. Despite the evident decline and negative outlook for the company, the investor might hold onto the stock, hoping for a miraculous recovery rather than reallocating the funds into more promising investments.

Another manifestation of the sunk cost fallacy is overinvestment in underperforming stocks. Investors may pour additional funds into a failing company, believing that a more significant investment will eventually turn things around. This approach often leads to deeper financial losses, as the initial investment bias clouds rational judgment.

An investor may continue to buy shares of a struggling company, convinced that they can average down their cost basis. While this strategy can be effective in certain circumstances, it becomes a fallacy when the underlying fundamentals of the company do not support a recovery.

In today's fast-paced market environment, information is readily available, making it easy for investors to fall prey to the sunk cost fallacy. News of a company's potential recovery or promising developments can reinforce the desire to hold onto losing investments, even when the situation has fundamentally changed.

If a company announces a new product line that generates initial excitement, investors may cling to their shares, believing that the stock will rise again. However, if the company's fundamentals remain weak, this hope can lead to greater losses.

To navigate the complexities of the stock market and mitigate the effects of the sunk cost fallacy, investors can adopt several strategies:

Setting clear criteria for buying and selling stocks can help mitigate emotional decision-making. By defining specific metrics for success, such as target prices or performance indicators, investors can approach their portfolios with a more objective mindset.

An investor might decide to sell a stock if its price falls

below a certain percentage of its purchase price, regardless of the initial investment. This approach creates a more disciplined investment strategy and reduces the likelihood of succumbing to the sunk cost fallacy.

Shifting focus from past investments to future potential can help break the cycle of the sunk cost fallacy. Investors should continually evaluate the fundamentals of their holdings, considering whether the stock has the potential for growth or if it is better to invest elsewhere.

This evaluation might involve analyzing company performance, market trends, and industry developments. By concentrating on the future outlook rather than past investments, investors can make more rational decisions.

The sunk cost fallacy poses a significant challenge for investors in the stock market, often leading to irrational decision-making and financial losses. By understanding the psychological mechanisms behind this bias and adopting strategies to overcome it, investors can make more informed decisions and enhance their overall investment performance.

Emphasizing objective evaluation, clear investment criteria, and regular reviews can help mitigate the emotional toll of past investments. Ultimately, recognizing and addressing the sunk cost fallacy is essential for navigating the complexities of the stock market and achieving long-term financial success.

PATIENCE AND DISCIPLINE: WINNING THE LONG GAME

Investing is a journey that requires more than just financial knowledge and an understanding of market trends; it necessitates the virtues of patience and discipline. While many investors are drawn to the allure of quick gains, the most successful investors understand that building wealth over time is often a slow, methodical process. This essay will explore the significance of patience and discipline in investing, the psychological barriers that can impede these qualities, and practical strategies for cultivating them in your investment journey.

Investing with a long-term perspective is essential for maximizing returns. Historically, the stock market has shown upward trends over extended periods, but it is also characterized by volatility and downturns. Investors who react impulsively to short-term market fluctuations often miss out on substantial gains. For example, during the 2008 financial crisis, many investors panicked and sold off their holdings, only to see the market recover and reach new heights within a few years.

Patience allows investors to withstand market volatility

and stay focused on their long-term goals. It enables them to maintain a steady course even when market conditions are unfavorable. When investors are patient, they are more likely to stick to their investment strategy, take advantage of lower prices during market downturns, and ultimately benefit from the compounding effects of long-term investments.

The concept of compounding is central to successful investing. Compounding occurs when the returns on an investment generate additional returns, leading to exponential growth over time. This phenomenon highlights the importance of patience in investing; the longer you leave your money invested, the more significant the compounding effect will be.

For instance, consider two investors: Investor A invests $10,000 at an annual return of 7% for 30 years, while Investor B invests the same amount but only for 15 years. Investor A's investment will grow to approximately $76,000, while Investor B will have around $28,000. The difference illustrates how time and patience can lead to substantial differences in investment outcomes.

Discipline in investing means sticking to a well-thought-out investment strategy, regardless of external influences. This involves setting clear investment goals, defining a risk tolerance, and choosing investment vehicles that align with those goals. A disciplined investor regularly reviews their portfolio, rebalances as necessary, and avoids impulsive decisions based on emotions or market noise.

One common mistake investors make is chasing trends or attempting to time the market. This often results in buying high and selling low, which is counterproductive. Disciplined investors understand that they should follow their strategy and make decisions based on research and analysis rather than emotions. This approach minimizes the risk of emotional trading and helps investors maintain a steady course through market fluctuations.

Discipline also involves effective risk management. Investors must understand their risk tolerance and develop strategies to manage it, including diversifying their portfolios, setting stop-loss orders, and avoiding over-leveraging. A disciplined approach to risk management helps investors avoid catastrophic losses that can occur from emotional decision-making or hasty reactions to market events.

Consider an investor who has a diversified portfolio across various asset classes. If one sector experiences a downturn, the investor's overall portfolio may still perform well due to the strength of other investments. This discipline in diversification can help mitigate losses and keep the investor on track toward their long-term financial goals.

Developing patience and discipline requires cultivating mindfulness and emotional awareness. Recognize when fear or greed influences your decision-making and take a step back to evaluate your emotions. Practicing mindfulness techniques, such as meditation or journaling, can help you develop a more balanced perspective and reduce impulsive reactions.

Regularly reviewing your investment portfolio and progress toward your goals is essential for maintaining discipline. Set periodic check-ins, such as quarterly or annually, to assess your performance and make necessary adjustments. This practice allows you to stay informed about your investments, helps you remain focused on your long-term goals, and reinforces the importance of patience.

Engaging with other investors can provide valuable insights and encouragement. Joining investment clubs or online forums can help you learn from the experiences of others and share your own journey. Being part of a supportive community can foster discipline and patience by holding you accountable to your investment strategy.

Investing is a constantly evolving field, and staying informed can help you make better decisions. Regularly reading books, attending workshops, or taking online courses can deepen your understanding of investing and reinforce the importance of patience and discipline. The more knowledgeable you are, the more confident you will feel in your investment decisions.

Cultivating a long-term perspective can help you resist the temptation to react impulsively to short-term market fluctuations. Focus on the big picture and remind yourself that investing is a marathon, not a sprint. Keeping your long-term goals in mind can help you stay patient and disciplined, even during challenging market conditions.

Successful investing is a journey that requires the development of patience and discipline. While the allure of quick gains can be tempting, the most successful investors understand that building wealth over time is often a slow and methodical process. By recognizing the importance of patience and discipline, understanding the psychological barriers that can impede these qualities, and implementing practical strategies to cultivate them, investors can enhance their ability to make informed decisions and achieve their long-term financial goals. In a world filled with market noise and fleeting trends, the virtues of patience and discipline remain timeless principles for successful investing.

COGNITIVE DISSONANCE

Cognitive dissonance is a psychological phenomenon that occurs when individuals hold two or more contradictory beliefs, values, or attitudes simultaneously. This discomfort can lead to significant stress, prompting individuals to find ways to alleviate this dissonance. In the context of investing, cognitive dissonance plays a crucial role as investors frequently encounter conflicting information and face decisions that may challenge their preconceived notions and beliefs. Understanding how investors reconcile these conflicts can shed light on their behavior, decision-making processes, and the dynamics of financial markets.

Cognitive dissonance theory, proposed by Leon Festinger in the late 1950s, posits that people have an inherent drive to maintain harmony among their beliefs, attitudes, and behaviors. When confronted with dissonance—such as when new information contradicts existing beliefs—individuals will experience psychological discomfort, which they are motivated to reduce. This can lead to a variety of coping mechanisms, including:

Change in beliefs or attitudes: Adjusting existing beliefs to align with new information.

Selective exposure: Seeking out information that supports existing beliefs while avoiding conflicting data.

Rationalization: Justifying decisions or beliefs despite contrary evidence.

Disregarding information: Dismissing information that contradicts one's beliefs.

Investing often involves navigating a landscape filled with uncertainty, ambiguity, and conflicting information. Investors frequently encounter new data, analyst opinions, market trends, and economic indicators that may contradict their existing beliefs about particular stocks, sectors, or market conditions. This environment can generate cognitive dissonance, as investors must reconcile their beliefs with new information to make informed decisions.

Investors regularly receive mixed signals about the performance of assets. For example, a company may report strong earnings while also facing negative news about legal issues or market competition. This duality can create discomfort as investors try to determine the true value and future potential of the investment.

Investors often exhibit confirmation bias, favoring information that confirms their pre-existing beliefs while dismissing evidence that contradicts them. This bias can lead to dissonance when investors encounter information that challenges their chosen investment thesis.

Investors may develop emotional attachments to specific stocks or investment strategies, making it challenging to adjust their beliefs in light of new evidence. The emotional investment can exacerbate cognitive dissonance, as admitting a mistake might also mean confronting feelings of regret or loss.

Many investors display overconfidence in their decision-making abilities, leading them to underestimate risks or ignore conflicting information. When faced with contrary evidence, this overconfidence can create dissonance, compelling investors to justify their decisions.

Investors use various strategies to reconcile cognitive dissonance when confronted with conflicting information. Understanding these strategies can illuminate the psychological processes underpinning investment decisions.

One common approach to resolving cognitive dissonance is reevaluating the conflicting information. Investors may scrutinize the data to find justifications for their beliefs. For instance, if an investor believes in a company's long-term potential but encounters negative news, they might analyze the context of that news—determining whether it is a short-term setback or indicative of a long-term trend. This reevaluation allows investors to maintain their original beliefs while accommodating the new information.

To reduce dissonance, investors often seek out information that reinforces their existing beliefs. This can involve reading analyst reports, news articles, or online forums that align with their perspectives. By surrounding themselves with supportive narratives, investors can diminish feelings of discomfort and bolster their confidence in their decisions. However, this strategy can also lead to confirmation bias, as investors selectively filter information to align with their preconceptions.

To counteract cognitive dissonance, some investors adopt a more holistic approach by diversifying their sources of information. By considering multiple viewpoints, they can mitigate the discomfort caused by conflicting data. For example, an investor might consult various analysts or financial experts to gain a more balanced understanding of a stock's performance. This exposure to diverse perspectives can help investors reconcile conflicting information and make more informed decisions.

Successful investors often exhibit flexibility and

adaptability in their decision-making processes. When faced with cognitive dissonance, these investors are more willing to reconsider their beliefs and strategies. They may set predefined thresholds for when to reevaluate their positions based on new information or market conditions. This adaptability allows them to navigate dissonance without becoming overly attached to their initial beliefs.

Cognitive dissonance can lead to heightened emotional responses, which can cloud judgment and decision-making. Investors who recognize this phenomenon often develop emotional regulation strategies to manage their feelings effectively. Techniques such as mindfulness, reflection, and stress management can help investors remain calm and objective when confronted with conflicting information. By regulating their emotions, investors can approach decisions with a clearer mindset.

A crucial aspect of investing is accepting uncertainty and the inherent risks involved. Investors who embrace this uncertainty are more likely to view conflicting information as part of the investment process rather than a threat to their beliefs. This mindset allows them to navigate dissonance with greater resilience, enabling them to make informed decisions despite the complexities of the market.

Cognitive dissonance plays a significant role in shaping investor behavior as individuals navigate the complexities of financial markets. The discomfort arising from conflicting information and beliefs can prompt various coping mechanisms, influencing decision-making processes. By understanding how investors reconcile dissonance, financial professionals can develop strategies to communicate more effectively with clients, helping them navigate uncertainty and make informed investment choices.

The ability to manage cognitive dissonance is essential for successful investing. As financial markets continue to evolve, investors who cultivate flexibility, emotional regulation, and a willingness to embrace uncertainty will be better equipped to thrive in an environment characterized by conflicting information and rapid change. Recognizing the psychological dynamics at play in investment decisions can enhance both individual investor success and the overall efficiency of financial markets.

BEHAVIORAL FINANCE

Behavioral finance is an essential subfield of finance that blends psychology with economics to understand how cognitive biases and emotional factors influence the financial decisions of investors and market participants. Unlike traditional finance, which assumes that investors are rational and markets are efficient, behavioral finance posits that human behavior is often irrational, leading to mispriced assets and market anomalies. This perspective is particularly relevant to the stock market, where investor psychology can create volatility, bubbles, and crashes. This paper will delve into the fundamental concepts of behavioral finance, explore various psychological biases that affect investor behavior, and examine their implications for stock market performance.

Prospect theory is a cornerstone of behavioral finance, emphasizing how individuals perceive gains and losses. According to this theory, people are loss-averse, meaning they experience the pain of losses more intensely than the pleasure of equivalent gains. This aversion to loss leads investors to make conservative decisions, such as holding onto losing stocks to avoid realizing losses, which can result in poor portfolio performance.

Mental accounting refers to the cognitive process by which individuals categorize and evaluate financial outcomes. Investors often separate their investments into distinct "accounts" based on their source or purpose, leading to irrational behavior. For example, an investor might treat a bonus from work differently from regular income, using it for riskier investments or indulgent purchases. This compartmentalization can distort decision-making and affect overall financial well-being.

Overconfidence bias occurs when individuals overestimate their knowledge, abilities, or control over events. In the stock market, overconfident investors may engage in excessive trading, believing they can predict market movements or select winning stocks based on limited information. Research has shown that overconfidence often leads to inferior investment performance, as these investors tend to ignore or downplay risks.

Herding behavior describes the tendency of individuals to follow the actions of a larger group, often neglecting their own information or analysis. This phenomenon is particularly evident in the stock market, where investors may buy or sell stocks based on popular trends rather than fundamental analysis. Herding can lead to asset bubbles, where prices soar due to collective enthusiasm, and subsequent crashes when the bubble bursts.

Anchoring is a cognitive bias where individuals rely heavily on the first piece of information they encounter when making decisions. In finance, this may manifest as an investor fixating on a stock's historical price or a specific valuation metric, affecting their judgment regarding future performance. For instance, an investor who bought a stock at a high price may hold onto it longer than warranted, hoping it will return to its previous value rather than objectively assessing its current worth.

Confirmation bias is the tendency to seek out information that confirms one's existing beliefs while ignoring contradictory evidence. In the context of the stock market, investors may only pay attention to news or analysis that supports their views on a particular stock, leading to skewed decision-making. This bias can reinforce erroneous beliefs and contribute to suboptimal investment choices.

Understanding behavioral biases is crucial for analyzing stock market dynamics. These biases can lead to mispricing of assets and create inefficiencies in the market.

Behavioral biases often contribute to increased market volatility. During periods of economic uncertainty or market downturns, fear and panic can trigger herding behavior, leading to mass sell-offs and sharp declines in stock prices. Conversely, during market rallies, overconfidence can drive excessive buying, pushing prices beyond their intrinsic value. This volatility can create opportunities for savvy investors who can identify mispriced assets.

Asset bubbles occur when prices of stocks or other assets rise rapidly beyond their fundamental value, fueled by investor optimism and herding behavior. The dot-com bubble of the late 1990s and the housing bubble leading up to the 2008 financial crisis are prime examples of how behavioral biases can create unsustainable market conditions. Once reality sets in, a shift in investor sentiment can lead to abrupt price corrections, resulting in significant financial losses for those caught in the bubble.

Behavioral biases can lead to a focus on short-term performance at the expense of long-term investment strategies. Investors may react emotionally to daily market fluctuations, causing them to buy high and sell low. This short-termism can be detrimental to long-term portfolio growth, as investors fail to remain committed to their original investment strategies.

The influence of psychological biases can distort investors' assessments of a company's fundamentals. For instance, overconfidence may lead investors to underestimate risks associated with a particular stock, while anchoring may cause them to disregard recent developments that impact a company's performance. As a result, investment decisions may be driven more by sentiment than by solid financial analysis.

Behavioral finance offers a profound understanding of how psychological factors influence stock market behavior and investment decisions. By recognizing the various cognitive biases and emotional influences that impact investor behavior, individuals can develop more effective investment strategies, reduce the impact of irrationality, and achieve better financial outcomes.

As the stock market continues to evolve and technology advances, the integration of behavioral finance insights into investment practices and regulatory frameworks will be crucial for fostering healthier markets. With a growing emphasis on financial literacy and investor protections, the principles of behavioral finance will play an increasingly important role in shaping the future of investing.

In an era marked by rapid information flow and technological advancements, understanding the nuances of human behavior will be key to navigating the complexities of the stock market. By embracing the lessons of behavioral finance, investors can strive for more rational decision-making, mitigate the effects of biases, and ultimately enhance their chances of long-term success in the ever-changing financial landscape.

MENTAL TOUGHNESS IN BEAR MARKETS

Bear markets, characterized by declining stock prices and widespread pessimism, can be particularly challenging for investors. They often evoke strong emotional responses, such as fear, anxiety, and uncertainty, which can lead to impulsive decisions and significant financial losses. Building resilience and emotional stability during these turbulent times is crucial for maintaining a healthy mindset and making rational investment choices. This section will explore the psychological aspects of bear markets, the importance of resilience, and practical strategies for cultivating emotional stability.

A bear market is generally defined as a decline of 20% or more in stock prices over an extended period, often accompanied by negative economic indicators and widespread investor pessimism. These market conditions can result from various factors, including economic recessions, geopolitical tensions, rising interest rates, and shifts in investor sentiment. Bear markets can be psychologically taxing for investors, leading to a range of emotional responses that may impact their financial decisions.

Investing is inherently emotional, and bear markets often amplify these feelings. Understanding the psychological aspects of investing during downturns can help individuals recognize their emotional responses and develop strategies to cope effectively.

One of the most common reactions during a bear market is fear. Investors may panic at the sight of declining asset values, leading them to make hasty decisions, such as selling off investments to avoid further losses. This reaction is often fueled by negative news cycles and social media commentary, which can exacerbate feelings of anxiety.

Behavioral finance research shows that individuals are generally more sensitive to losses than gains. This phenomenon, known as loss aversion, can be particularly pronounced during bear markets. Investors may hold onto losing positions longer than necessary, hoping for a turnaround, while simultaneously selling profitable investments too early due to fear of potential declines.

In times of uncertainty, investors may be inclined to follow the crowd, leading to herding behavior. This can result in mass sell-offs or panic buying, further exacerbating market volatility. Understanding this tendency can help investors recognize when they are being influenced by the actions of others rather than relying on their analysis.

Investors often experience cognitive dissonance during bear markets, where their beliefs about the market clash with the reality of declining prices. This dissonance can create feelings of discomfort and lead to poor decision-making, as individuals may struggle to reconcile their expectations with actual outcomes.

Some investors may initially react to bear markets with overconfidence, believing they can time the market or identify undervalued assets. This overestimation of one's abilities can lead to poor investment choices and increased risk-taking.

Building resilience is essential for navigating the

challenges posed by bear markets. Resilience refers to the ability to adapt and bounce back from adversity, and it plays a crucial role in maintaining emotional stability during turbulent times.

Resilient investors are better equipped to maintain a long-term perspective during bear markets. They understand that market fluctuations are a natural part of the investment cycle and can separate short-term volatility from long-term investment goals.

Resilience enables investors to make more rational and informed decisions. By managing their emotions and maintaining a clear head, resilient investors are less likely to succumb to panic selling or emotional decision-making.

Resilient individuals view challenges as opportunities for growth. By reflecting on their experiences during bear markets, investors can learn valuable lessons that inform their future decision-making and risk management strategies.

Building resilience contributes to overall emotional well-being. Resilient investors are better equipped to cope with stress and anxiety, leading to improved mental health and a more positive outlook during difficult market conditions.

Emotional awareness is the ability to recognize and understand one's emotions. By cultivating emotional awareness, investors can identify their emotional responses to market fluctuations and take steps to manage them effectively.

In bear markets, it's essential to focus on factors within one's control rather than getting caught up in external uncertainties. By concentrating on controllable aspects, investors can reduce feelings of helplessness and anxiety.

Investing requires patience and discipline, particularly during bear markets when emotions may run high. Developing a disciplined approach can help investors avoid impulsive decisions and stay committed to their long-term strategies.

Flexibility and adaptability are essential traits for navigating the uncertainties of bear markets. Investors should be willing to adjust their strategies and approaches as needed while maintaining a commitment to their long-term goals.

A growth mindset is the belief that abilities and intelligence can be developed through effort and learning. Cultivating a growth mindset can help investors embrace challenges and setbacks as opportunities for growth rather than viewing them as insurmountable obstacles.

Visualization is a powerful technique that can help investors mentally prepare for market fluctuations and cultivate emotional stability. By envisioning positive outcomes and successful navigation of bear markets, investors can build confidence and resilience.

Maintaining emotional stability during bear markets requires attention to self-care. Taking care of one's physical, mental, and emotional well-being can enhance resilience and provide a strong foundation for effective decision-making.

In the age of information, constant exposure to negative news about market conditions can exacerbate anxiety and fear. Being selective about the sources of information and limiting exposure to negative headlines can contribute to emotional stability.

After a bear market has passed, take the time to reflect on your experiences and reassess your investment strategies. Reflecting on past behaviors and decisions can provide insights for future investing and help reinforce resilience.

Navigating bear markets requires resilience and emotional stability. By understanding the psychological aspects of investing, developing effective strategies, and practicing self-care, investors can build a strong foundation to withstand market fluctuations. Cultivating a long-term perspective, practicing emotional awareness, and seeking support can significantly enhance an investor's ability to thrive during challenging market conditions.

As markets inevitably fluctuate, building resilience is not just about surviving bear markets but also about emerging stronger and more informed. By embracing the lessons learned during downturns and committing to personal growth, investors can foster emotional stability and position themselves for long-term success. Ultimately, the journey through bear markets can serve as a valuable opportunity for growth, learning, and enhanced emotional intelligence in the world of investing.

EMOTIONAL INTELLIGENCE FOR SMART INVESTING

Emotional intelligence is a crucial aspect of personal and professional success, especially in high-stakes environments such as the stock market. It encompasses the ability to recognize, understand, and manage our own emotions, as well as the emotions of others. In the context of investing, emotional intelligence plays a pivotal role in decision-making, risk management, and long-term strategy development. This essay explores the relationship between emotional intelligence and investing in the stock market, discussing how it can enhance investment performance, improve decision-making, and foster a healthy investment mindset.

Emotional intelligence consists of several key components:

Self-awareness: The ability to recognize one's emotions and their effects on thoughts and behavior.

Self-regulation: The ability to manage emotions, impulses, and resources effectively.

Motivation: The drive to pursue goals with energy and persistence, often influenced by emotional factors.

Empathy: The ability to understand and share the feelings of others, which is vital in building relationships and networks.

Social skills: The ability to manage relationships and navigate social complexities effectively.

Investing in the stock market is not merely a numbers game; it's an emotional journey that involves navigating volatility, uncertainty, and risk. Emotional intelligence can help investors make rational decisions and avoid the pitfalls that come from emotional reactions to market fluctuations.

Investors often face situations where they must make quick decisions based on rapidly changing market conditions. Emotional intelligence allows individuals to remain calm and focused under pressure, enabling them to analyze situations objectively rather than reacting impulsively. During a market downturn, emotionally intelligent investors are less likely to panic and sell their assets at a loss. Instead, they can assess the situation, consider their long-term goals, and make informed decisions about whether to hold, buy, or sell.

Investing inherently involves risk, and emotional intelligence can enhance an investor's ability to assess and manage that risk. By understanding their own emotional responses to risk—whether fear, greed, or anxiety—investors can develop strategies to mitigate those feelings. For example, a self-aware investor may recognize that their fear of loss is driving them to sell off investments prematurely. By practicing self-regulation, they can create a plan that aligns with their risk tolerance and investment objectives, allowing them to stay the course during turbulent times.

Emotional intelligence encourages a long-term perspective on investing, which is crucial for success in the stock market. Many investors struggle with short-term thinking, reacting to daily market movements and noise rather than focusing on their long-term goals. An emotionally intelligent investor recognizes that markets fluctuate and that patience is essential for realizing gains over time. By cultivating motivation and persistence, they are more likely to stick to their investment strategies and resist the temptation to chase trends or make impulsive trades.

The stock market is influenced by the emotions of countless investors, leading to phenomena like market bubbles and crashes. Emotionally intelligent investors can recognize when market sentiment is irrational, allowing them to make decisions based on fundamentals rather than emotions. For example, during a market bubble, when prices are driven by hype rather than intrinsic value, an emotionally intelligent investor may be more inclined to take profits or avoid new investments, whereas less emotionally aware investors may become swept up in the frenzy.

In addition to individual decision-making, emotional intelligence plays a significant role in building relationships and networks within the investing community. Investors often rely on advice, insights, and partnerships to make informed decisions. Empathy and social skills facilitate effective communication and collaboration, helping investors establish trust with advisors, peers, and other stakeholders. By understanding the emotions and motivations of others, emotionally intelligent investors can engage in more fruitful discussions, gain diverse perspectives, and enhance their decision-making processes.

While some individuals may naturally possess higher levels of emotional intelligence, it is a skill that can be developed over time.

Emotional intelligence is a vital component of successful investing in the stock market. By enhancing decision-making, risk management, and long-term perspective, emotional intelligence empowers investors to navigate the complexities of the market with greater confidence and resilience. Developing emotional intelligence is an ongoing process that requires self-awareness, reflection, and continuous learning. As investors cultivate these skills, they can enhance their performance and ultimately achieve their financial goals.

Investing is not just about numbers; it's about understanding the emotional landscape of oneself and the market. Emotionally intelligent investors are better equipped to manage the challenges that arise, enabling them to thrive in an ever-changing financial environment. In a world where markets can be unpredictable, emotional intelligence serves as a guiding compass, helping investors remain focused on their long-term objectives while skillfully navigating the emotional highs and lows of investing.

THE PSYCHOLOGY OF LONG-TERM INVESTING

Investing in the stock market is not solely a financial endeavor; it is also a deeply psychological one. While market trends, economic indicators, and company fundamentals play crucial roles in investment success, the mental and emotional aspects of investing are equally important. Long-term investing, in particular, requires a robust psychological framework to navigate the inevitable ups and downs of the market. This essay explores the psychology of long-term investing, including the emotional and cognitive factors that influence investor behavior, the importance of discipline and patience, and strategies for cultivating a long-term investment mindset.

Long-term investing involves holding assets for an extended period, typically years or even decades, with the goal of capital appreciation, income generation, or both. This strategy contrasts sharply with short-term trading, which relies on market timing and rapid decision-making. Long-term investors often focus on fundamental analysis, seeking undervalued stocks, growth potential, and steady income sources. The psychological challenges of long-term investing include managing emotional reactions to market fluctuations, resisting the temptation to react impulsively, and maintaining a focus on long-term goals despite short-term market noise.

A successful long-term investor must cultivate a mindset that prioritizes patience and discipline. This mindset is essential for weathering market volatility and adhering to a long-term investment strategy. Long-term investing requires a willingness to forgo short-term gains in favor of sustainable growth over time.

Long-term investors should set realistic expectations regarding returns and market behavior. While historical data may suggest that equities have generally provided strong returns over the long run, it is essential to acknowledge that past performance is not indicative of future results. Setting realistic expectations helps mitigate the disappointment and frustration that can arise from underperformance or market corrections.

Investors should also recognize that market cycles can last for several years, and periods of downturn may be followed by periods of recovery. Understanding this cyclical nature of the market can help investors maintain their composure and resist the urge to react impulsively during downturns.

One of the most compelling arguments for long-term investing is the power of compounding. Compounding occurs when investment returns generate additional returns over time, leading to exponential growth. The earlier an investor begins to invest, the more pronounced the effects of compounding can be. This understanding reinforces the importance of patience and discipline in long-term investing.

Long-term investors can cultivate a mindset that embraces compounding by regularly contributing to their investment accounts, reinvesting dividends, and staying committed to their investment strategy, even during market downturns. By focusing on the potential long-term benefits of compounding, investors can remain motivated and resilient in the face of short-term volatility.

The psychology of long-term investing is a complex interplay of emotions, cognitive biases, and mental discipline. Successful long-term investors must cultivate self-awareness, patience, and a disciplined approach to navigate the inevitable market fluctuations. By understanding and addressing the emotional and psychological challenges of investing, individuals can develop a robust investment mindset that supports their long-term goals.

Investing is not merely a financial transaction; it is a journey that requires mental fortitude, resilience, and a commitment to continuous learning. By embracing the principles of long-term investing and building a supportive environment, investors can increase their chances of achieving lasting financial success while navigating the emotional landscape of the markets. Ultimately, cultivating a healthy psychological approach to long-term investing can empower individuals to make informed, rational decisions that align with their financial aspirations and goals.

THE PAIN OF REGRET

Investing in the stock market is often characterized as a rational endeavor, driven by analytical skills and market research. However, a closer look reveals that emotions play a significant role in investor behavior, particularly regret. Regret is an emotional response that can arise when individuals feel they have made a poor decision or missed an opportunity. In the context of investing, this emotion can profoundly influence decision-making processes, leading to behaviors that may not align with rational investment strategies. This essay explores the multifaceted impact of regret on investments in the stock market, examining its psychological underpinnings, manifestations, and strategies to mitigate its effects.

Regret is a complex emotional response that arises when individuals perceive that their current situation could have been improved had they made a different choice. It often involves feelings of sadness, disappointment, and frustration about past decisions, and it can lead to a desire to avoid similar mistakes in the future. In investing, regret is particularly pronounced due to the significant financial implications of investment decisions, where missed opportunities or poor choices can result in substantial monetary losses.

The psychological basis of regret is rooted in the concept of counterfactual thinking, which refers to the mental process of imagining alternative scenarios or outcomes that could have occurred had a different decision been made. This process can lead investors to ruminate on their choices, comparing the actual outcomes with hypothetical ones, which can intensify feelings of regret. For instance, if an investor sells a stock that subsequently increases in value, they may experience regret for not holding onto the investment, leading to feelings of disappointment and frustration.

Regret aversion theory suggests that individuals tend to avoid decisions that may lead to feelings of regret. This theory posits that the fear of experiencing regret can influence decision-making processes, leading to more conservative or risk-averse behavior. In the context of investing, regret aversion can cause investors to shy away from certain opportunities, fearing that they may make a poor choice that they will later regret. This tendency can result in missed investment opportunities or the reluctance to sell underperforming assets.

One of the most significant impacts of regret on investment behavior is the tendency to overreact to market movements. When investors experience regret over previous decisions, they may become overly sensitive to short-term fluctuations in the market. This sensitivity can lead to impulsive decision-making, where investors buy or sell stocks based on emotional reactions rather than careful analysis.

Regret can also contribute to herding behavior, where investors follow the actions of others rather than relying on their research or analysis. This tendency often stems from a fear of missing out (FOMO) on profitable opportunities or a desire to avoid being the only investor left behind. When investors observe others profiting from certain investments, they may experience regret for not participating and decide to follow the crowd, even if it contradicts their original investment strategy.

Herding behavior can lead to market bubbles, where inflated stock prices result from widespread buying based on emotional reactions rather than fundamental analysis. Once the bubble bursts, those who followed the herd may experience heightened regret for their decisions, leading to further emotional turmoil and potentially irrational behavior in the future.

Regret can also manifest as an unwillingness to sell losing investments. Investors may hold onto underperforming stocks due to fear of realizing a loss, which can lead to a phenomenon known as the "sunk cost fallacy." This fallacy occurs when individuals continue to invest in a losing asset because they have already incurred costs, hoping that the stock will eventually rebound.

Regret can lead to emotional decision-making, where investors prioritize their feelings over rational analysis. Emotional decision-making can result in impulsive choices, such as buying or selling stocks based on short-term price movements or news headlines rather than conducting thorough research. This approach can lead to suboptimal investment outcomes and increased portfolio volatility.

Investors may find themselves making decisions driven by emotions rather than adhering to a well-defined investment strategy. This emotional rollercoaster can lead to a cycle of buying high and selling low, further exacerbating feelings of regret.

The experience of regret can significantly impact an investor's risk tolerance. Individuals who have experienced significant losses may become more risk-averse, fearing further losses and avoiding investments that carry higher risks. This shift in risk tolerance can lead to overly conservative investment strategies, potentially limiting growth opportunities.

Some investors may react to regret by taking on excessive risk in an attempt to recoup losses, leading to impulsive and potentially reckless investment decisions. Striking a balance between risk tolerance and the influence of regret is crucial for long-term investment success.

Regret can have a lasting impact on future investment choices. When investors experience regret over a specific decision, they may be more hesitant to engage in similar investments in the future. This hesitancy can lead to missed opportunities, as investors may avoid stocks or sectors that previously resulted in regretful outcomes.

Regret is a powerful emotion that can significantly impact investment behavior in the stock market. Understanding the psychological underpinnings of regret, its manifestations, and its influence on decision-making is essential for investors seeking long-term success. By recognizing the effects of regret on their choices, investors can develop strategies to mitigate its impact and cultivate a more rational approach to investing.

Embracing a long-term perspective, establishing a structured investment plan, practicing self-reflection, limiting information overload, and seeking professional guidance are all effective strategies for managing the emotional challenges associated with regret. By implementing these strategies, investors can enhance their decision-making processes, reduce impulsive behaviors, and ultimately achieve their financial goals.

THE ROLE OF EGO IN INVESTING

Investing in the stock market is often portrayed as a rational and analytical process, primarily driven by data, trends, and economic indicators. However, the psychological aspects of investing, particularly pride and self-perception, play a significant role in shaping investor behavior. These emotions can influence decision-making processes, leading to choices that may not align with sound investment principles. This essay explores the impact of pride and self-perception on investment decisions, examining how these factors can lead to poor outcomes and strategies to mitigate their influence.

Pride is a complex emotion that can manifest in various forms, from a healthy sense of self-esteem to an inflated sense of superiority. In the context of investing, pride can lead investors to overestimate their abilities and knowledge, fostering a sense of invincibility that may cloud judgment. When investors allow pride to dictate their decisions, they may take unnecessary risks, ignore sound advice, or refuse to acknowledge mistakes.

Self-perception refers to the way individuals view themselves, including their abilities, attributes, and worth. This perception can significantly influence decision-making processes in the stock market. Investors with a strong self-perception may feel confident in their abilities to analyze stocks and predict market trends. However, this confidence can quickly turn into overconfidence, leading to hasty decisions and potential losses.

Self-perception also affects how investors react to feedback and criticism. Those with a positive self-perception may struggle to accept constructive criticism or recognize their limitations, leading to a reluctance to adjust their strategies or seek help when needed.

One of the most significant ways pride can hinder sound investment decisions is through overconfidence. When investors feel overly confident in their abilities, they may underestimate risks, ignore important information, and overcommit to their positions. This overconfidence can lead to a series of poor decisions that ultimately impact their portfolio's performance.

Pride can lead investors to believe that they possess superior knowledge or skills compared to others. This perception may result in a reluctance to diversify their portfolios, as they may feel that they can select individual stocks that will outperform the market. By concentrating their investments in a few stocks, investors expose themselves to higher risks, as the failure of any single investment can significantly impact their overall returns.

Pride can create a barrier to learning and growth, particularly when it comes to accepting feedback or criticism. Investors who view themselves as experts may resist input from others, dismissing valuable advice that could enhance their decision-making processes. This resistance can lead to a lack of adaptability and an unwillingness to learn from past mistakes.

Pride can also lead investors to engage in loss-chasing behavior, where they attempt to recover losses by investing in riskier assets or making impulsive trades. This behavior often stems from a desire to prove their abilities and regain lost capital, rather than making sound, rational decisions based on analysis.

Self-perception can lead to confirmation bias, where investors seek information that supports their preexisting beliefs while ignoring contradictory evidence. Investors with a strong self-perception may feel justified in their decisions and selectively filter information that aligns with their views. This bias can hinder objective analysis and lead to misguided investment choices.

Self-perception can influence how investors respond to market volatility and emotional triggers. Investors with a positive self-perception may experience heightened confidence during bull markets, leading to more aggressive investment strategies. Conversely, during bear markets, they may struggle to accept losses, leading to emotional decision-making that prioritizes feelings over rational analysis.

Self-perception plays a critical role in shaping an investor's risk tolerance. Investors who view themselves as knowledgeable and capable may take on more risk than is appropriate for their financial situation or investment goals. This overestimation of their abilities can lead to investments that do not align with their risk tolerance, ultimately resulting in negative outcomes.

One of the most effective ways to mitigate the impact of pride on investment decisions is to cultivate humility. Investors should recognize that the stock market is inherently uncertain, and even the most knowledgeable individuals can make mistakes. Embracing humility allows investors to remain open to feedback, learn from their experiences, and adapt their strategies accordingly.

Practicing humility can involve acknowledging past mistakes and seeking input from others, whether through discussions with financial advisors, engaging with investment communities, or participating in educational seminars. By embracing a growth mindset, investors can enhance their decision-making processes and improve their investment outcomes.

Developing emotional awareness is crucial for understanding how pride and self-perception influence investment decisions. Investors should regularly reflect on their emotions and consider how these feelings may be affecting their decision-making processes. This self-awareness can help investors recognize when pride or overconfidence is clouding their judgment.

Investors should prioritize education and continuous learning to enhance their understanding of the stock market and improve their decision-making processes. This commitment to learning fosters a growth mindset and helps investors recognize their limitations, reducing the influence of pride and self-perception.

Pride and self-perception are powerful emotions that can significantly hinder sound investment decisions in the stock market. Overconfidence, confirmation bias, emotional decision-making, and a reluctance to seek feedback are just a few ways these factors can negatively impact investor behavior. Recognizing the influence of pride and self-perception is essential for investors seeking to improve their decision-making processes and achieve long-term success.

By cultivating humility, establishing a structured investment plan, seeking diverse perspectives, fostering emotional awareness, and emphasizing continuous learning, investors can mitigate the impact of pride and self-perception on their investment choices. Embracing a more balanced and rational approach to investing can lead to improved decision-making, reduced emotional turmoil, and greater financial success.

Investing is a journey that requires not only analytical skills but also emotional intelligence and self-awareness.

By understanding and managing the psychological factors that influence their decisions, investors can navigate the complexities of the stock market with confidence and clarity. Ultimately, recognizing the potential pitfalls of pride and self-perception can empower investors to make informed choices that align with their financial goals and aspirations.

TIME HORIZONS

Investing in the stock market is often framed as a calculated endeavor, driven by financial metrics and market analysis. However, beneath the surface lies a complex interplay of psychological factors that significantly influence investment strategies. One of the most critical psychological factors is the timeframe in which investors perceive their investment goals. Psychological timeframes can affect decision-making, risk tolerance, and ultimately, the success or failure of investment strategies. This essay explores the various ways psychological timeframes shape investment strategies, the implications for investors, and strategies to align psychological timeframes with financial objectives.

Psychological timeframes refer to the mental constructs individuals use to evaluate their experiences and make decisions regarding the future. These timeframes can be short-term, medium-term, or long-term and significantly influence how individuals perceive risk, reward, and the consequences of their actions. In investing, psychological timeframes shape how investors view their portfolios, make trading decisions, and react to market movements.

Time perspective is a psychological concept that refers to how individuals perceive and relate to time. This perspective can be categorized into various dimensions, including past, present, and future orientations. Each dimension can influence decision-making processes differently:

Past Orientation: Individuals with a strong past orientation may dwell on previous investment successes or failures, leading them to either repeat past mistakes or become overly conservative in their decisions. For example, an investor who lost money during a market downturn may become hesitant to invest again, influenced by their past experiences.

Present Orientation: Investors with a present-time focus may prioritize immediate gains and losses, leading to impulsive trading behavior. This orientation can result in overreacting to short-term market fluctuations, resulting in a lack of strategic planning and poor investment decisions.

Future Orientation: A future-oriented perspective encourages individuals to think about long-term consequences and investment goals. Investors with a future focus are more likely to adopt disciplined, long-term strategies and resist the temptation to make hasty decisions based on short-term market movements.

Psychological timeframes can significantly influence how investors make decisions. For instance, investors with short-term timeframes may prioritize quick gains, leading them to engage in frequent trading or speculate on volatile stocks. Conversely, those with long-term timeframes are more likely to adopt a buy-and-hold strategy, focusing on fundamental analysis and the long-term growth potential of their investments.

Short-term investors are more susceptible to market noise and emotional reactions, leading to heightened volatility in their portfolios. They may react impulsively to news events, earnings reports, or technical indicators, resulting in frequent buying and selling.

Short-term investors may chase past performance, investing in stocks that have recently performed well without considering underlying fundamentals. This behavior can lead to the "herd mentality," where investors flock to popular stocks, inflating prices and increasing risk.

Short-term investors may engage in higher-risk strategies, seeking quick returns. This propensity for risk can lead to significant losses if the market moves against them, especially if they are not adequately prepared for volatility.

Investors with a medium-term perspective often balance short-term gains with a longer-term vision. Medium-term investors may employ tactical asset allocation strategies, adjusting their portfolios based on market conditions while still maintaining a long-term focus. This approach allows them to capitalize on market opportunities without abandoning their overall investment strategy.

Investors with a medium-term perspective may be more attuned to market trends, using technical analysis to inform their decisions. While they seek to capture short- to medium-term movements, they also consider broader economic and fundamental factors. Medium-term investors often exhibit greater flexibility in their strategies, allowing them to adapt to changing market conditions while maintaining a commitment to their long-term goals.

Long-term investors prioritize sustainable growth and the compounding of returns over extended periods. Long-term investors often adopt a buy-and-hold approach, focusing on quality investments that align with their financial goals. They are less likely to react to short-term market fluctuations and are more inclined to weather volatility. Long-term investors prioritize fundamental analysis, assessing the financial health, competitive positioning, and growth potential of companies. This focus allows them to make informed investment decisions based on intrinsic value rather than short-term price movements. Investors with a long-term perspective are generally more emotionally resilient, able to withstand market downturns without panicking. This resilience enables them to stick to their investment strategies even during periods of heightened volatility.

Psychological timeframes also play a crucial role in shaping investors' risk tolerance. Investors with short-term timeframes may perceive risk differently than those with long-term perspectives. Investors with short-term timeframes may view market fluctuations as more threatening, leading to a heightened sensitivity to losses. This perception can result in conservative strategies that limit exposure to volatility but may also sacrifice potential gains. Long-term investors are generally more willing to accept short-term volatility in pursuit of long-term gains. They recognize that market downturns are a natural part of the investment cycle and maintain a focus on their overall financial objectives.

Understanding how psychological timeframes influence investment strategies is critical for investors seeking to align their behaviors with their financial goals.

Setting clear investment objectives based on realistic timeframes is essential for aligning psychological perspectives with financial goals.

Psychological timeframes play a crucial role in shaping investment strategies, influencing how investors perceive risk, make decisions, and react to market movements. Short-term, medium-term, and long-term perspectives each carry unique implications for investor behavior and outcomes. Understanding these psychological timeframes is essential for investors seeking to align their actions with their financial goals.

By recognizing the impact of emotional responses and behavioral biases, investors can adopt strategies to mitigate their influence. Establishing clear investment objectives, implementing a diversified investment strategy, practicing mindfulness, seeking professional guidance, and utilizing technology can enhance decision-making processes and improve overall investment outcomes.

Aligning psychological timeframes with investment strategies is a journey that requires self-awareness, discipline, and a commitment to continuous learning. By understanding their psychological timeframes, investors can navigate the complexities of the stock market more effectively, making informed choices that lead to long-term financial success. The integration of psychological insights into investment strategies not only fosters better decision-making but also promotes emotional resilience, empowering investors to achieve their financial aspirations while effectively managing the psychological challenges inherent in investing.

THE PARADOX OF CHOICE

The stock market is often regarded as a domain of opportunity, where investors can build wealth, secure their financial futures, and achieve personal goals. However, the myriad options available in this arena can lead to a phenomenon known as the "paradox of choice." The concept suggests that while having choices is generally viewed as a good thing, an overwhelming number of options can lead to feelings of anxiety, paralysis, and dissatisfaction. In the context of the stock market, this paradox can profoundly influence investment behavior, decision-making processes, and overall financial outcomes. This essay delves into the paradox of choice as it relates to the stock market, exploring its implications, effects on investor behavior, and strategies to navigate this complexity.

The paradox of choice refers to the phenomenon where an abundance of options can lead to negative psychological consequences. While having choices can enhance individual freedom and autonomy, too many options can result in feelings of overwhelm, anxiety, and regret. Schwartz argues that the increase in choice can lead to a paradoxical decline in overall satisfaction, as individuals grapple with the complexities of making decisions.

When faced with numerous options, individuals may

struggle to process information effectively. Cognitive overload occurs when the brain is tasked with evaluating too many variables, leading to indecision and anxiety. In the stock market, investors may find it challenging to analyze various investment opportunities, resulting in delays or avoidance in decision-making.

Maximizers seek the best possible option, often leading them to explore every possible choice exhaustively. This approach can lead to disappointment and regret when the chosen option does not meet their expectations. In contrast, satisficers settle for "good enough" options, which can lead to greater satisfaction but may also result in missed opportunities.

The fear of making the wrong choice can exacerbate the paradox of choice. When faced with multiple investment opportunities, investors may worry about potential losses or missed gains. This fear can lead to paralysis, where investors become reluctant to make any decisions, further compounding their stress and uncertainty.

In a world of abundant choices, individuals often engage in social comparisons, evaluating their decisions against those of others. This tendency can lead to feelings of inadequacy and dissatisfaction, as investors may feel pressured to select options that align with perceived norms or trends, rather than their own financial goals and values.

The paradox of choice has significant implications for investor behavior and decision-making in the stock market.

The overwhelming number of available investment options can lead to increased anxiety among investors. This stress may stem from concerns about making the wrong choice, leading to emotional decision-making rather than rational analysis. As anxiety mounts, investors may avoid making decisions altogether, missing out on potential opportunities.

Cognitive overload can lead to indecision, where

investors find it challenging to commit to a particular investment strategy. This indecision may result in procrastination, as individuals delay taking action while they continue to weigh their options. In fast-moving markets, procrastination can be detrimental, as opportunities may quickly disappear.

The abundance of choices may encourage a short-term focus, with investors fixating on immediate gains rather than long-term objectives. This tendency can lead to impulsive trading behaviors, as investors react to market fluctuations instead of adhering to a well-defined investment strategy. Consequently, the likelihood of making poor decisions increases, ultimately undermining long-term financial success.

The paradox of choice can contribute to overtrading, where investors buy and sell securities frequently in an attempt to capitalize on various opportunities. This behavior is often driven by the desire to explore every available option, leading to increased transaction costs and reduced overall returns.

While diversification is a fundamental principle of sound investing, the paradox of choice can complicate this strategy. Investors may struggle to strike the right balance between diversifying their portfolios and maintaining simplicity.

In an effort to mitigate risk, investors may become overzealous in their diversification strategies, creating portfolios with too many holdings. Over-diversification can dilute potential returns and make it challenging to monitor individual investments effectively. The desire to explore every option can lead to a fragmented approach that lacks coherence.

When faced with numerous investment options, investors may lose sight of their core holdings, becoming distracted by peripheral choices. This lack of focus can result in insufficient attention to the performance of key investments, potentially hindering overall portfolio growth.

The complexity of evaluating numerous investment choices can lead to inadequate risk assessment. Investors may struggle to understand the specific risks associated with each option, making it difficult to construct a well-balanced portfolio that aligns with their risk tolerance.

Reducing the number of investment options can alleviate feelings of overwhelm and facilitate decision-making. Focusing on quality investments rather than an abundance of options can enhance decision-making.

The paradox of choice profoundly impacts investors in the stock market, highlighting the intricate relationship between human psychology and financial decision-making. While having access to a diverse array of investment options is often seen as beneficial, it can also lead to cognitive overload, anxiety, and indecision. Investors may find themselves paralyzed by the sheer volume of choices, struggling to make informed decisions that align with their financial goals.

Understanding the psychological mechanisms behind the paradox of choice allows investors to navigate these challenges more effectively. By setting clear investment objectives, limiting their options, prioritizing quality over quantity, practicing mindfulness, and seeking professional guidance, individuals can mitigate the negative effects of choice overload.

Fostering a disciplined and strategic approach to investing can help individuals overcome the emotional and psychological hurdles associated with the paradox of choice. By acknowledging the complexities of human behavior in the context of investing, individuals can make more informed and rational decisions, leading to greater satisfaction and success in their financial endeavors. In a landscape where the right choice can feel elusive, clarity, focus, and self-awareness are essential tools for achieving long-term investment goals.

ENDOWMENT EFFECT

The endowment effect is a cognitive bias that plays a significant role in decision-making and economic behavior, particularly in the realm of investing. It refers to the phenomenon where individuals assign a higher value to things merely because they own them, leading to a discrepancy between perceived value and actual market value. This psychological tendency can have profound implications for investors, causing them to overestimate the worth of their holdings and influencing their trading behavior, asset allocation, and overall investment strategy. Understanding the endowment effect is crucial for investors seeking to optimize their financial decisions and achieve better investment outcomes. This essay explores the endowment effect, its psychological underpinnings, its impact on investor behavior, and strategies to mitigate its influence.

The endowment effect is a behavioral economic principle that suggests that individuals value an item more highly when they own it compared to when they do not. This bias can lead individuals to hold onto assets longer than rational economic analysis would dictate. The term was popularized by Richard Thaler, a leading figure in behavioral economics, who conducted various experiments illustrating this phenomenon.

Ownership often becomes intertwined with personal identity and self-concept. When individuals acquire an asset, they may view it as an extension of themselves, leading to an emotional attachment that skews their perception of its value. This attachment can cause investors to overestimate the worth of their holdings, as they perceive them not just as financial assets but as integral components of their lives.

The status quo bias refers to the tendency for individuals to prefer the current state of affairs over change. This bias can lead investors to cling to their existing holdings, overvaluing them relative to new investment opportunities. The comfort of familiarity can reinforce the endowment effect, causing investors to underestimate potential risks and overestimate the benefits of maintaining their current positions.

One of the most significant consequences of the endowment effect is that investors often overestimate the value of their holdings.

Investors may hesitate to sell underperforming assets, convinced that their intrinsic value is higher than the market reflects. This behavior can lead to missed opportunities for reallocating capital to more promising investments, ultimately hindering portfolio performance.

The endowment effect can contribute to a reluctance to diversify portfolios. Investors may be overly attached to their current holdings, viewing them as superior investments compared to potential new opportunities. This lack of diversification increases portfolio risk and may expose investors to greater volatility.

Emotional attachment to owned assets can lead to impulsive trading decisions. Investors may react irrationally to market fluctuations, holding onto losing positions longer than warranted or selling winning positions prematurely due to fear of loss. Such emotional trading behaviors can undermine long-term investment strategies and result in suboptimal financial outcomes.

Overestimating the value of certain assets may lead to misallocation of resources within a portfolio. Investors may allocate more capital to overvalued holdings while neglecting undervalued opportunities. This misallocation can prevent investors from maximizing their overall returns.

The endowment effect not only affects individual investors but can also have broader implications for market behavior.

The endowment effect contributes to market inefficiencies, as overvalued assets may persist in the market due to investors' reluctance to sell. This can result in mispricing and increased volatility, as the disparity between perceived and actual value creates discrepancies in supply and demand.

The endowment effect can exacerbate asset bubbles, as investors hold onto overvalued assets, believing they will continue to appreciate. This behavior can lead to inflated prices and increased risk of subsequent crashes when the market corrects.

The emotional nature of the endowment effect may also contribute to herd behavior in the market. When investors become overly attached to their holdings, they may follow the crowd, exacerbating trends and contributing to market swings.

The endowment effect is a powerful cognitive bias that influences how investors perceive the value of their holdings, often leading to overestimation and emotional decision-making. Understanding the psychological mechanisms behind the endowment effect is essential for investors seeking to optimize their financial decisions and achieve better investment outcomes.

By recognizing the impact of loss aversion, ownership identity, and other cognitive biases, investors can adopt strategies to mitigate the endowment effect's influence on their behavior. Establishing clear decision-making frameworks, seeking external perspectives, focusing on long-term goals, and increasing awareness of behavioral finance principles can empower investors to make more rational and objective decisions.

Navigating the complexities of the endowment effect requires self-awareness, discipline, and a commitment to continuous learning. By cultivating a more objective approach to valuing their holdings, investors can enhance their overall financial performance, avoid pitfalls associated with emotional attachment, and make informed choices that align with their long-term objectives. Understanding the endowment effect is not just an academic exercise; it is a critical step towards achieving financial success in the dynamic and often unpredictable world of investing.

THE PSYCHOLOGY OF PREDICTIONS

Predictions play a fundamental role in various fields, from finance and economics to healthcare and climate science. In a world characterized by uncertainty, the ability to forecast future events can lead to better decision-making and strategic planning. However, the psychology underlying predictions can significantly impact their accuracy. One pervasive psychological phenomenon that affects predictions is optimism bias. This bias can cloud market forecasts, leading to overly positive expectations and potentially costly misjudgments. This essay will explore the psychology of predictions, delve into the concept of optimism bias, and analyze how this bias influences market forecasts.

Predictions are inherently uncertain. They are often based on past data, trends, and expert opinions, but they can never be guaranteed. The act of predicting involves cognitive processes that are influenced by individual beliefs, emotions, and social dynamics. Researchers have identified various factors that can affect the accuracy of predictions.

Cognitive biases are systematic patterns of deviation from norm or rationality in judgment. They can lead individuals to rely on heuristics or mental shortcuts that simplify complex information, sometimes resulting in flawed conclusions.

The opinions and behaviors of peers, experts, and social groups can shape individual predictions. Groupthink, for example, can lead to a consensus that overlooks dissenting opinions, resulting in overly optimistic forecasts.

Emotions can significantly influence decision-making. Fear, anxiety, and excitement can skew perceptions of risk and opportunity, leading to biased predictions.

In an era of abundant information, individuals may struggle to process all available data, leading them to rely on simplistic narratives or trends that may not accurately reflect reality.

Optimism bias refers to the tendency for individuals to overestimate the likelihood of positive outcomes while underestimating the potential for negative events. This bias is pervasive across various domains, from personal life choices to professional decisions. Key characteristics of optimism bias include:

Illusion of Control: Individuals often believe they can influence outcomes more than they realistically can. This illusion can lead to overconfidence in predictions and riskier behaviors.

Positive Outcome Expectation: Optimism bias leads people to expect positive results from their decisions, often ignoring or downplaying the possibility of adverse consequences.

Selective Attention: Individuals may focus on information that supports their optimistic views while disregarding data that contradicts their beliefs. This selective attention can skew predictions and reinforce biases.

Resilience to Feedback: When faced with negative feedback or outcomes that contradict their predictions, individuals may rationalize or minimize the implications rather than adjust their beliefs.

Optimism bias can lead to a systematic neglect of risks in market forecasts. Analysts and investors may focus primarily on potential upside scenarios while underestimating the likelihood of negative developments. This was evident during the subprime mortgage crisis when many financial institutions underestimated the risks associated with housing market declines, leading to significant losses.

Optimism bias can distort individuals' perceptions of time horizons when making predictions. Investors may believe that positive trends will continue indefinitely, leading them to overlook cyclical patterns or economic indicators suggesting a potential downturn. This distortion can lead to poor investment decisions, as individuals fail to adequately assess the long-term sustainability of their predictions.

Traditional forecasting models often rely on rational assumptions about market behavior. However, incorporating behavioral insights can enhance the accuracy of predictions. For example, models that account for investor sentiment and behavioral biases can provide a more realistic view of market dynamics.

The psychology of predictions is complex and influenced by various cognitive biases, with optimism bias being particularly impactful. This bias can cloud market forecasts, leading to overvaluation of assets, herd behavior, neglect of risks, and distorted time horizons. Understanding the role of optimism bias is crucial for improving the accuracy of predictions in financial markets. By integrating insights from behavioral finance, individuals and organizations can develop strategies to mitigate the influence of optimism bias, leading to more informed decision-making and ultimately more resilient markets. In an uncertain world, recognizing and addressing our cognitive biases is essential for navigating the complexities of prediction and ensuring that we do not succumb to the allure of unchecked optimism.

THE ROLLERCOASTER OF EMOTIONS

Investing in financial markets can be an emotionally charged endeavor, especially during periods of volatility. Market fluctuations often evoke a range of emotions, from euphoria during bull markets to fear and panic during downturns. Understanding and managing these emotional responses is crucial for investors to make informed decisions and maintain their long-term investment strategies. This essay explores the emotional ups and downs of a volatile market, examining the psychological factors that influence investor behavior and offering practical strategies for handling these emotions effectively.

Market volatility refers to the degree of variation in the price of financial instruments over time. High volatility indicates significant price swings, while low volatility suggests more stable price movements. Volatile markets can arise from various factors, including economic indicators, geopolitical events, interest rate changes, and investor sentiment. Understanding the nature of volatility is essential for investors to navigate its emotional impact.

In the early stages of a bull market, investors may experience a sense of euphoria. As prices rise and portfolios gain value, greed can set in, leading to overconfidence and risky investment behaviors. This phase is often characterized by a "fear of missing out" (FOMO), where investors feel compelled to buy into rising markets without thoroughly assessing the risks.

As volatility increases, uncertainty can creep in. Investors may feel anxious about potential downturns, leading them to question their investment strategies. This anxiety can be compounded by news reports, social media, and conversations with peers, creating a cycle of fear and worry.

When markets decline sharply, panic can set in. Many investors may react impulsively, selling off assets to minimize perceived losses. This behavior is often driven by loss aversion, a psychological phenomenon where individuals prefer to avoid losses rather than acquire equivalent gains. The fear of losing money can lead to irrational decision-making and may result in selling at the worst possible time.

Following significant market downturns, investors may feel a sense of despair and regret. Those who sold in a panic may lament their decisions, wishing they had held on to their investments. This emotional state can lead to a reluctance to re-enter the market, even when conditions improve.

Eventually, some investors may come to terms with their losses and accept the cyclical nature of markets. This phase often involves a reassessment of investment goals and strategies. While recovery may take time, it can also present opportunities for learning and growth.

Successfully navigating the emotional ups and downs of a volatile market requires a proactive approach.

Market volatility can be a valuable learning experience. Instead of viewing downturns solely as negative events, investors can use these periods to evaluate their strategies, understand market dynamics, and enhance their investment knowledge. Embracing a growth mindset allows individuals to approach challenges with curiosity rather than fear.

Handling the emotional ups and downs of a volatile market is a critical skill for investors. By understanding the psychological factors that influence emotional responses and employing effective strategies, individuals can navigate market fluctuations with greater resilience. Developing a clear investment plan, maintaining a long-term perspective, and practicing mindfulness are just a few of the strategies that can help investors manage their emotions effectively.

As markets continue to evolve, it's essential for investors to remain adaptable and open to learning from their experiences. By embracing the challenges posed by volatility, individuals can foster a deeper understanding of their emotional triggers and enhance their overall investment journey. Ultimately, the ability to manage emotions in the face of market volatility can lead to more informed decision-making, greater confidence, and a more successful investment experience.

THE DANGERS OF PERFECTIONISM

Perfectionism is often viewed as a desirable trait, associated with high standards and an unwavering commitment to excellence. In many fields, striving for perfection can lead to remarkable achievements. However, in the context of investing, perfectionism can become a double-edged sword. While the desire to make flawless investment decisions may seem prudent, it can lead to a range of negative consequences that undermine financial success and emotional well-being. This essay explores the dangers of perfectionism in investing, examining its psychological roots, its impact on decision-making, and strategies for fostering a healthier approach to investment.

Perfectionism is characterized by a relentless pursuit of flawlessness and a fear of making mistakes. Perfectionists often set exceedingly high standards for themselves and experience significant distress when they perceive that they have fallen short of those standards.

All-or-Nothing Thinking: Perfectionists tend to view situations in black-and-white terms, believing that anything less than perfect is unacceptable. This mindset can lead to extreme reactions to performance outcomes, fostering anxiety and self-doubt.

Fear of Failure: Perfectionists are often paralyzed by the fear of failure. This fear can result in avoidance behaviors, where individuals refuse to take risks or make decisions due to the possibility of negative outcomes.

Self-Criticism: Perfectionists are typically harsh self-critics. They may internalize failures or perceived shortcomings, leading to a cycle of negative self-talk that undermines confidence and motivation.

Overemphasis on Control: Many perfectionists believe that they can control all aspects of a situation. This need for control can lead to frustration and anxiety when faced with uncertainty or unexpected developments.

Individuals with self-oriented perfectionism impose high standards on themselves and strive to achieve them. They may be motivated by personal goals but are often driven by fear of failure.

This type involves imposing high expectations on others. Individuals with other-oriented perfectionism may criticize colleagues, friends, or family members for not meeting their standards.

This form arises from the perception that others expect perfection. Individuals may feel pressure to conform to societal standards, leading to heightened anxiety and stress.

Perfectionism is often fueled by cognitive distortions, which are irrational thought patterns that distort reality. Common cognitive distortions associated with perfectionism include:

Catastrophizing: This involves imagining the worst possible outcome in any situation. For investors, this may manifest as fearing catastrophic losses or market crashes, leading to avoidance of potentially profitable opportunities.

Overgeneralization: Perfectionists may view one setback as

evidence of a broader failure. For example, a poor investment decision may lead to the belief that they will never succeed in investing, causing them to abandon their strategies altogether.

Should Statements: Perfectionists often use "should" statements to impose unrealistic expectations on themselves. For instance, they may think, "I should always make the right investment decision," leading to feelings of inadequacy when they do not meet this expectation.

Cultural factors can also contribute to perfectionism. Societies that prioritize achievement, success, and competitiveness can create an environment where individuals feel compelled to strive for perfection. This pressure can be particularly pronounced in the context of investing, where performance is often scrutinized, and success is highly valued.

One of the most significant dangers of perfectionism in investing is paralyzed decision-making. Perfectionists may become so fixated on making the "perfect" investment choice that they fail to act altogether. This can lead to missed opportunities, especially in fast-moving markets where timely decisions are crucial. The fear of making a mistake can create analysis paralysis, preventing investors from executing their strategies.

Perfectionists often engage in extensive research and analysis to ensure that they are making the best possible decision. While due diligence is essential in investing, an excessive focus on gathering information can lead to analysis paralysis. Investors may become overwhelmed by the sheer volume of data, second-guessing their strategies and delaying action. This information overload can create a false sense of security, leading to indecision and missed opportunities.

Perfectionists may avoid taking risks altogether, fearing that any misstep could lead to failure. This risk aversion can result in overly conservative investment strategies that prioritize safety over potential gains. While it is essential to manage risk, an avoidance mindset can limit growth opportunities and lead to stagnant portfolios.

The internal pressure perfectionists place on themselves can lead to heightened levels of stress and anxiety. When investors experience losses or setbacks, they may engage in harsh self-criticism, blaming themselves for their perceived failures. This emotional distress can cloud judgment and lead to impulsive decisions, further exacerbating the situation.

Perfectionism can lead to an aversion to diversification, as perfectionists may seek to invest only in what they perceive as "perfect" opportunities. This narrow focus can expose investors to significant risks if their chosen investments underperform. In contrast, a diversified portfolio can help mitigate risks and provide more stable returns over time.

Perfectionism can contribute to detrimental behavioral patterns, such as overtrading or frequent portfolio adjustments. Investors may feel compelled to constantly tweak their holdings in pursuit of the "perfect" portfolio, leading to increased transaction costs and potentially lower overall returns. This behavior can be counterproductive, as it often distracts from the long-term investment strategy.

Recognizing that imperfection is a natural aspect of investing can help alleviate the pressure to achieve flawless results. Investors should view mistakes as valuable learning opportunities rather than failures. Embracing imperfection can lead to greater resilience and adaptability in the face of market challenges.

Perfectionism can pose significant dangers in the realm of investing, leading to paralyzed decision-making, emotional distress, and detrimental behaviors. While the desire for flawless investment decisions may seem noble, it can hinder an investor's ability to navigate the complexities of the market effectively. By recognizing the psychological roots of perfectionism and implementing strategies to foster a healthier mindset, investors can develop a more balanced approach to investing.

By embracing imperfection, setting realistic expectations, and focusing on long-term goals, investors can mitigate the negative impact of perfectionism and enhance their chances of financial success. Ultimately, a shift in perspective from striving for perfection to pursuing growth and learning can empower investors to make more informed, confident decisions in an ever-changing market.

SCARCITY MENTALITY

Scarcity mentality, often referred to as a "scarcity mindset," is a psychological phenomenon characterized by the belief that resources are limited and that there is never enough to go around. This mindset can manifest in various aspects of life, including financial decisions, relationships, and even career choices. In the realm of investing, a scarcity mentality can lead to distorted decision-making and suboptimal investment strategies. This essay delves into the nature of scarcity mentality, its psychological roots, its impact on decision-making in the stock market, and strategies to overcome this mindset for better investment outcomes.

Scarcity mentality refers to the belief that there is not enough of something to satisfy one's needs or desires. This can encompass various resources, such as time, money, opportunities, or even social connections.

Individuals with a scarcity mindset often fear missing out on opportunities, leading them to make impulsive decisions based on the perceived urgency of acquiring limited resources. A scarcity mentality can lead to an exaggerated focus on potential losses rather than potential gains. This heightened sense of loss aversion can result in overly conservative investment strategies. Scarcity-minded individuals may prioritize short-term gains over long-term growth, leading to hasty decisions that could undermine their overall investment strategy. Scarcity mentality fosters a competitive mindset, where individuals feel they must compete with others for limited resources. This can lead to increased anxiety and stress.

From an evolutionary perspective, humans have developed survival instincts that prioritize the acquisition of resources. In a world where resources are limited, individuals have learned to be cautious and protective of what they have.

Scarcity mentality is often exacerbated by cognitive biases, such as loss aversion and the availability heuristic. Loss aversion refers to the tendency to prioritize avoiding losses over acquiring equivalent gains, while the availability heuristic leads individuals to rely on readily available information when making decisions.

Cultural and societal factors can also contribute to the development of a scarcity mentality. Societies that emphasize competition and individualism may foster a belief in limited resources, further entrenching scarcity-minded thinking.

Scarcity mentality can also lead to an exaggerated focus on potential losses. Investors who fear losing money may adopt overly conservative strategies that limit their potential for growth.

Scarcity-minded investors may avoid taking calculated risks altogether, leading to a lack of diversification in their portfolios. This can result in missed opportunities for growth in high-potential investments.

Fear of losing money can prompt investors to sell stocks prematurely when they experience short-term fluctuations in price. This reactive behavior can lead to selling assets at a loss rather than holding them for potential long-term gains.

When investors focus excessively on loss aversion, they may fail to recognize undervalued assets or investment opportunities. This can prevent them from capitalizing on favorable market conditions.

Investors driven by scarcity mentality may chase short-term trends rather than conducting thorough research and analysis. This can lead to impulsive trading decisions based on market hype rather than sound investment principles.

The urgency to capitalize on perceived limited opportunities can result in insufficient research and analysis. Investors may make decisions based on incomplete information, increasing the likelihood of poor outcomes.

When investors focus on short-term gains, they may lose sight of their long-term financial goals. This can result in a lack of strategic planning and an inability to achieve desired outcomes over time.

Scarcity mentality fosters a competitive mindset, where investors feel they must compete with others for limited resources. This competition can lead to several detrimental behaviors:

Investors may view others as competitors rather than collaborators, hindering their ability to build valuable relationships within the investment community. This lack of networking can limit access to valuable information and opportunities.

The belief in limited resources can create pressure to outperform others. This pressure may lead to reckless investment decisions as individuals strive to keep up with perceived competitors.

Scarcity mentality can foster a sense of isolation, where investors feel they must navigate the market alone. This isolation can prevent them from seeking support, advice, and collaboration that could enhance their investment strategies.

The fear of limited resources can take a significant toll on mental health. Scarcity mentality can lead to heightened levels of stress and anxiety, which can further distort decision-making in the stock market.

The constant worry about missing out on opportunities or experiencing losses can lead to chronic stress. This stress can impair cognitive function and decision-making abilities, resulting in suboptimal investment choices.

Heightened stress and anxiety can lead to emotional decision-making, where investors react impulsively rather than relying on rational analysis. This can result in hasty trades and poor investment outcomes.

The pressure to constantly seek opportunities and compete can lead to burnout. Investors may feel overwhelmed and exhausted, resulting in disengagement from the market or poor decision-making.

Scarcity mentality can diminish overall satisfaction with investments and financial success.

Investors may constantly compare their performance to others, leading to feelings of inadequacy and dissatisfaction. This constant comparison can prevent individuals from appreciating their achievements.

The focus on what is lacking can overshadow the recognition of accomplishments. Investors may fail to celebrate their successes, leading to diminished motivation and engagement.

A scarcity mindset can lead to a lack of gratitude for what one has. This mindset may prevent individuals from acknowledging the resources and opportunities available to them.

One of the most effective ways to combat scarcity mentality is to cultivate an abundance mindset, which is characterized by the belief that there are ample opportunities and resources available.

Scarcity mentality can profoundly impact decision-making in the stock market, leading to distorted perceptions of risk and reward. The fear of limited resources and opportunities can result in impulsive decisions, an exaggerated focus on losses, and a short-term mindset. Understanding the psychological roots of scarcity mentality and its impact on investment behavior is essential for developing more effective investment strategies.

By cultivating an abundance mindset, developing a long-term perspective, and implementing strategies to limit information overload, investors can overcome the challenges posed by scarcity mentality. Building a supportive network of fellow investors and seeking professional guidance can also enhance confidence and promote better decision-making.

Recognizing the detrimental effects of scarcity mentality and adopting a more balanced, proactive approach to investing can lead to more successful outcomes and greater satisfaction in the financial journey. Investing is not merely about the resources at hand; it is also about the mindset with which individuals approach the market and the opportunities that abound.

GROUPTHINK: WHEN CONSENSUS LEADS TO CATASTROPHE

In the ever-evolving world of finance and investing, individuals are often confronted with a plethora of opinions and analyses. These perspectives can come from various sources, including financial experts, analysts, social media, and even friends and family. While it is natural for investors to seek guidance from others, aligning too closely with group opinions can pose significant psychological risks. This essay explores the nature of groupthink in the market, the psychological factors that contribute to this behavior, and the potential consequences of such alignment. Furthermore, it offers strategies for maintaining independent decision-making to mitigate the psychological risks associated with group consensus.

Groupthink is a psychological phenomenon where individuals prioritize consensus and harmony over critical evaluation and independent thought. In the context of the stock market, this can manifest as investors aligning their decisions with popular trends or prevailing opinions, often at the expense of their own analysis and judgment. Key characteristics of groupthink include:

Illusion of Invulnerability: Group members may develop an inflated sense of confidence in their decisions, believing that their collective wisdom guarantees success.

Collective Rationalization: Individuals may dismiss warnings or contradictory information that could challenge the group's consensus. This rationalization can lead to poor decision-making.

Pressure to Conform: Group members may feel pressure to conform to the prevailing opinions, fearing social rejection or criticism if they voice dissenting views.

Self-Censorship: Individuals may withhold their opinions or doubts about the group's decisions to maintain harmony, resulting in a lack of diverse perspectives.

Cognitive dissonance is the mental discomfort experienced when individuals hold conflicting beliefs or when their actions contradict their values. To alleviate this discomfort, individuals may choose to align their opinions with the group, even if they have reservations about the prevailing sentiment. This can result in:

Compromised Decision-Making: Investors may make choices that do not align with their own research or analysis, leading to regret and poor performance.

Justification of Flawed Decisions: When the group consensus leads to negative outcomes, individuals may rationalize their decisions to reduce feelings of guilt or anxiety.

Social identity theory posits that individuals derive a sense of self from their group memberships. In the context of investing, this can lead to an overemphasis on group opinions as individuals seek validation and belonging. Key implications include:

Increased Risk-Taking: Individuals may take on more significant risks when investing with a group, driven by a desire to conform and maintain their social identity.

Resistance to Dissent: Fear of alienation from the group can prevent individuals from voicing concerns or questioning group decisions, ultimately undermining critical thinking.

Investors may develop an illusion of knowledge when they align closely with group opinions. This phenomenon occurs when individuals believe they possess more information than they actually do, leading to overconfidence in their decisions. Consequences include:

Overtrading: Investors may engage in excessive trading based on popular sentiment, incurring unnecessary transaction costs and potentially losing money.

Neglect of Fundamentals: The belief that group opinions are sufficient for decision-making can lead to a disregard for fundamental analysis, ultimately compromising investment success.

Aligning too closely with group opinions can lead to poor investment decisions characterized by a lack of critical evaluation. Key examples include:

Chasing Trends: Investors may buy into popular stocks or sectors without conducting thorough analysis, resulting in purchases at inflated prices and subsequent losses when trends reverse.

Ignoring Red Flags: The pressure to conform can cause individuals to overlook warning signs or red flags in a company or market, leading to financial losses.

The emotional toll of groupthink can be significant for investors. This distress may manifest in various ways:

Fear and Anxiety: Constantly aligning with group opinions can lead to heightened anxiety, particularly during market downturns. Investors may feel paralyzed by fear and uncertainty, leading to hasty decisions.

Loss of Confidence: Experiencing losses due to groupthink can erode an investor's confidence, making them more susceptible to future herd behavior and less willing to trust their judgment.

Aligning too closely with group opinions can lead to diminished satisfaction with investment outcomes. This may occur through:

Unrealized Potential: Investors may miss opportunities to achieve better returns by adhering to groupthink, resulting in dissatisfaction with their overall performance.

Regret and Frustration: When group decisions lead to losses, individuals may experience regret and frustration, ultimately impacting their future investment strategies.

Encouraging independent thinking is crucial for mitigating the psychological risks of aligning too closely with group opinions:

Conduct Personal Research: Investors should prioritize conducting their research and analysis rather than solely relying on group opinions. This empowers individuals to make informed decisions based on their findings.

Challenge Assumptions: Investors should regularly question their assumptions and beliefs, particularly when they align with prevailing opinions. This critical thinking can help uncover blind spots and lead to more balanced decision-making.

Engaging with diverse perspectives can enhance decision-making and reduce the risks associated with groupthink.

Investors should seek information from a variety of sources, including contrarian viewpoints, to develop a well-rounded understanding of market dynamics.

Participating in discussions with others who hold different opinions can foster constructive debate and encourage critical evaluation of prevailing sentiments.

Aligning too closely with group opinions in the market poses significant psychological risks for investors. The tendency toward groupthink can lead to poor decision-making, emotional distress, and diminished satisfaction with investment outcomes. By understanding the psychological factors that contribute to groupthink and the historical examples of its impact, investors can take proactive steps to mitigate these risks.

Fostering independent thinking, seeking diverse perspectives, establishing clear investment principles, and limiting exposure to social media are essential strategies for maintaining independent decision-making. Ultimately, by recognizing the dangers of aligning too closely with group opinions, investors can cultivate a more balanced and informed approach to investing, enhancing their chances of achieving long-term financial success. In a world where information is abundant and opinions abound, the ability to think critically and independently remains a valuable asset for any investor.

THE IMPACT OF NEWS ON INVESTOR PSYCHOLOGY

In today's fast-paced financial markets, news has become one of the most significant drivers of investor psychology and behavior. Information, whether disseminated through traditional media, social media platforms, or financial news networks, can greatly influence market sentiment, shape perceptions of value, and trigger emotional reactions among investors. Understanding the impact of news on investor psychology is crucial for both individual investors and financial professionals. This essay delves into the ways in which news affects investor behavior, the psychological mechanisms involved, the implications of news-driven trading, and strategies for investors to navigate the influence of news on their decision-making processes.

The impact of news on investor psychology can be classified into several categories:

Economic News: Reports on economic indicators such as GDP growth, unemployment rates, inflation, and consumer spending can significantly influence market sentiment. Positive economic news typically boosts investor confidence, while negative news can lead to panic and selling.

Corporate News: Earnings reports, management changes, product launches, and scandals are all types of corporate news that can directly impact stock prices. Positive corporate news may lead to a surge in stock prices, while negative news can cause sharp declines.

Geopolitical Events: Political developments, international relations, and crises can also influence investor sentiment. Events such as elections, trade negotiations, and military conflicts can lead to uncertainty and volatility in the markets.

Market Sentiment and Trends: News can shape market sentiment, often resulting in trends that drive collective investor behavior. For example, news about a tech breakthrough may lead to increased investment in technology stocks, while concerns about a recession can result in a broader market sell-off.

In the digital age, investors are bombarded with a constant flow of information. While access to news can empower investors, it can also lead to information overload, which has several psychological effects:

Analysis Paralysis: Faced with too much information, investors may struggle to make decisions, leading to inaction or delayed responses to market changes.

Emotional Decision-Making: Overexposure to news can heighten emotional responses, leading investors to make impulsive decisions driven by fear or greed rather than rational analysis.

Confirmation Bias: Investors may selectively focus on news that confirms their existing beliefs or opinions, further entrenching their positions and disregarding contradictory information.

Investor behavior is often driven by two primary emotions: fear and greed. News plays a significant role in amplifying these emotions:

Fear: Negative news, such as economic downturns or corporate scandals, can evoke fear among investors. This fear can lead to panic selling, where investors react hastily to news without fully assessing its implications.

Greed: Conversely, positive news can trigger greed, prompting investors to chase returns and take on excessive risks. This can lead to bubbles, where asset prices become detached from their intrinsic values.

Earnings reports are critical events for investors, as they provide insight into a company's financial health. The psychological impact of these reports can be profound:

Expectations vs. Reality: If a company's earnings report exceeds expectations, it can lead to euphoria among investors, resulting in a surge in stock prices. Conversely, disappointing earnings can trigger panic and selling.

Long-Term vs. Short-Term Focus: Investors may react emotionally to earnings reports without considering the long-term implications. Short-term fluctuations can overshadow fundamental analysis, leading to irrational trading behavior.

Geopolitical events, such as elections or international conflicts, can create significant volatility in financial markets:

Uncertainty and Anxiety: News of geopolitical tensions can create uncertainty, leading to increased volatility as investors react to the potential impact on global markets.

Sector-Specific Impact: Certain sectors may be more sensitive to geopolitical events, leading to disproportionate movements in stocks based on news related to those events.

One of the most significant implications of news-driven trading is the shift in focus from long-term investment strategies to short-term speculation:

Frequent Trading: Investors may engage in frequent trading

based on news, leading to higher transaction costs and potential tax implications. This short-term focus can undermine long-term investment strategies.

Neglect of Fundamentals: Constantly reacting to news can result in a disregard for fundamental analysis, as investors prioritize immediate reactions over long-term value assessments.

News-driven trading can contribute to increased volatility in financial markets:

Exaggerated Reactions: Investors may overreact to news, leading to sharp price movements that do not accurately reflect underlying fundamentals. This can create inefficiencies in the market.

Feedback Loops: The reaction of investors to news can create feedback loops, where initial price movements trigger further trading activity, amplifying volatility and market fluctuations.

The impact of news on investor psychology is profound, influencing behavior, decision-making, and market dynamics. The interplay of emotions such as fear and greed, the herd mentality, and cognitive dissonance can lead to irrational behavior and poor investment outcomes. While news is an essential aspect of the financial landscape, it is crucial for investors to develop strategies to navigate its influence effectively.

By establishing clear investment strategies, practicing emotional regulation, limiting exposure to news, and engaging in continuous education, investors can mitigate the psychological risks associated with news-driven trading. Ultimately, the ability to maintain a disciplined approach amidst the noise of news is essential for achieving long-term investment success. In a world where information is abundant and constantly evolving, understanding the psychological impact of news is a valuable skill that can empower investors to make informed decisions and achieve their financial goals.

BEHAVIORAL TRAPS: AVOIDING COMMON PSYCHOLOGICAL PITFALLS

Investing is as much a psychological endeavor as it is a financial one. Investors are often guided by emotions, cognitive biases, and mental errors that can lead to suboptimal decisions and significant financial losses. Recognizing and understanding these biases is crucial for developing a more rational approach to investing. This essay delves into the common biases and mental errors that investors face, explores their psychological underpinnings, and offers strategies for recognizing and avoiding these pitfalls to improve decision-making and achieve better investment outcomes.
Status quo bias is the preference for the current state of affairs, leading individuals to avoid change or new alternatives.

Investors may hold onto underperforming assets out of a reluctance to change their portfolios, resulting in missed opportunities for better returns.

This bias can perpetuate poor investment choices and hinder diversification.

Mental accounting refers to the tendency for individuals to categorize and treat money differently depending on its source or intended use.

Investors may treat profits from one investment differently from losses in another, leading to suboptimal portfolio management.

This can create a fragmented approach to investing, where decisions are made based on mental categories rather than overall financial health.

Evaluate all investments and financial resources together, considering the overall portfolio rather than focusing on isolated gains or losses.

Consider the potential returns of all investment opportunities rather than viewing them in silos, fostering a more comprehensive investment strategy.

Recognizing and avoiding common biases and mental errors in investing is crucial for achieving long-term financial success. By understanding the psychological underpinnings of biases such as overconfidence, loss aversion, and confirmation bias, investors can develop strategies to mitigate their influence on decision-making. Implementing structured decision-making processes, seeking diverse perspectives, and prioritizing continuous education can help investors cultivate a more rational and disciplined approach to investing.

The journey of investing is not just about financial acumen; it also involves mastering the psychological aspects that can significantly impact outcomes. By fostering self-awareness, emotional regulation, and a commitment to ongoing learning, investors can navigate the complexities of the market with greater confidence and achieve their financial goals. In a landscape where cognitive biases are prevalent, the ability to recognize and manage these influences remains a critical skill for successful investing.

THE DUNNING-KRUGER EFFECT: OVERESTIMATING YOUR SKILLS

The stock market is a complex ecosystem influenced by a myriad of factors, from economic indicators to psychological phenomena. One of the most significant psychological effects impacting investor behavior is the Dunning-Kruger Effect. Named after social psychologists David Dunning and Justin Kruger, this cognitive bias describes a phenomenon where individuals with low ability at a task overestimate their competence, while those with high ability often underestimate their competence. In the context of investing, the Dunning-Kruger Effect can lead to poor decision-making, overconfidence, and ultimately financial losses. This essay explores the Dunning-Kruger Effect, its implications in the stock market, and strategies for investors to mitigate its influence.

The Dunning-Kruger Effect is a cognitive bias that occurs when individuals with limited knowledge or experience in a specific domain overestimate their ability and knowledge. Conversely, those who are more knowledgeable often underestimate their competence. This paradox arises from a lack of metacognitive skills, which are necessary for accurate self-assessment.

The phenomenon was first described by Dunning and Kruger in their 1999 study published in the Journal of Personality and Social Psychology. They found that participants who performed poorly on tests of humor, grammar, and logic rated their performance significantly higher than it actually was. The study concluded that a lack of knowledge in a given area prevented individuals from accurately assessing their competence, leading to inflated self-perceptions.

Individuals with low ability often lack the metacognitive skills necessary to evaluate their performance accurately. They are unaware of what they do not know, leading to overconfidence. Cognitive biases, such as confirmation bias and hindsight bias, can exacerbate the Dunning-Kruger Effect. For instance, individuals may seek information that confirms their beliefs while ignoring contradictory evidence. People often assess their abilities relative to others. Those with limited skills may compare themselves to less competent individuals, further inflating their self-perception.

The Dunning-Kruger Effect can manifest in various ways within the stock market:

Overestimation of Knowledge: Investors who lack experience may believe they possess superior knowledge of the market. This overconfidence can lead to reckless trading, frequent buying and selling, and an inability to recognize when they are wrong.

Ignoring Expert Advice: Novice investors may disregard the insights of seasoned professionals, believing their understanding of market trends is sufficient. This can result in poor investment choices based on insufficient information.

Impulsive Decision-Making: Overconfident investors may react impulsively to market news or trends, leading to knee-jerk reactions rather than thoughtful analysis. This behavior can contribute to market volatility and loss of capital.

The presence of the Dunning-Kruger Effect in the stock market can contribute to increased volatility. When inexperienced investors act on overconfidence, their buying and selling behaviors can create sudden price swings, affecting overall market stability.

The tendency for less knowledgeable investors to drive prices up based on inflated perceptions can lead to asset bubbles. As prices rise, more inexperienced investors may jump in, further inflating the bubble until it inevitably bursts.

Conversely, when market sentiment shifts, overconfident investors may panic and sell off their holdings, exacerbating downturns and contributing to market crashes.

The Dunning-Kruger Effect can lead to the mispricing of assets in the market. When a significant number of investors overestimate their knowledge and abilities, it can distort valuations:

Overconfident investors may overlook fundamental analysis in favor of short-term trends or speculative opportunities. This can lead to inflated valuations for certain stocks, creating inefficiencies in the market.

As more inexperienced investors enter the market, their collective behavior can reinforce mispricing. When these investors react to price changes rather than fundamentals, it can create feedback loops that further distort valuations.

The Dunning-Kruger Effect presents a significant challenge for investors navigating the complexities of the stock market. By understanding this cognitive bias and its implications, investors can take proactive steps to mitigate its influence on their decision-making processes. Recognizing the limitations of one's knowledge, embracing lifelong learning, and adopting disciplined investment strategies are essential for overcoming overconfidence and improving investment outcomes.

In a market where emotions and biases often drive behavior, cultivating self-awareness and seeking professional guidance can help investors make more rational decisions. By acknowledging the Dunning-Kruger Effect and its impact on investing, individuals can enhance their financial literacy, develop a more informed approach to investing, and ultimately achieve greater success in the stock market. In a world of uncertainty, knowledge and humility remain the greatest assets for navigating the complexities of investing.

SURVIVOR BIAS: LEARNING FROM THE WINNERS WHILE IGNORING THE LOSERS

When we think about investing, successful investors like Warren Buffet, Peter Lynch, and Ray Dalio often come to mind. Their stories, books, and advice dominate the financial world. However, focusing exclusively on these individuals can give us a distorted view of the real risks involved in investing. Success stories captivate and inspire us, but they can create a biased understanding of how markets truly operate, masking the potential downsides. This selective focus on successful investors leaves out critical information about failure, which is often just as important in understanding market dynamics.

We will explore how this selective focus on the most successful investors can lead to a misinterpretation of market risks. We'll delve into the psychological biases that shape this phenomenon, discuss the importance of failure in investing, and highlight the hidden risks that often go unnoticed when we focus only on those who have succeeded.

One of the most prominent reasons why focusing on successful investors skews our understanding of market risks is a psychological bias known as "survivorship bias." Survivorship bias occurs when we concentrate on the people or things that survived a process while overlooking those that did not. In the world of investing, this means focusing on the investors who have made fortunes and ignoring those who have failed or gone unnoticed.

The financial media tends to lionize those who have amassed great wealth through investing. Books and documentaries are created about their strategies and habits, but the many investors who lost money or didn't achieve fame are often forgotten. This skewed representation makes it appear as though success in investing is more predictable or easier than it actually is.

While Warren Buffet's investment strategy has certainly been successful, there are many other investors who followed similar strategies but did not achieve anywhere near the same level of success. By ignoring the failures, we may mistakenly conclude that investing in the stock market is a straightforward path to wealth, when in reality it is fraught with risks that have led many to financial ruin.

Focusing solely on successful investors can also lead to a misunderstanding of the true nature of market risks. Many successful investors have stories of taking calculated risks that paid off, but the narrative often fails to mention the luck or timing involved. It can create an illusion that with the right strategy, market risks can be fully controlled or avoided.

This leads to overconfidence among retail investors, who may believe that by simply following the strategies of successful investors, they too can avoid significant losses. Overconfidence is a dangerous mindset in investing, as it can cause investors to overlook the inherent volatility of markets. They may take on more risk than they can handle, believing that they are following a proven formula.

Moreover, successful investors often have access to tools and resources that the average retail investor does not. They may have teams of analysts, years of experience, and large amounts of capital, all of which provide them with a safety net that smaller investors lack. By focusing only on these success stories, individual investors might underestimate the risks they face and overestimate their ability to replicate the same outcomes.

Failure is an integral part of the investing process, but it is often overlooked in favor of success stories. However, studying failure is just as important as studying success because it provides a more realistic view of the risks involved in investing. Understanding why certain investors fail can help individuals avoid making the same mistakes and can highlight the unpredictability of financial markets.

Many investors fail because of factors beyond their control, such as economic downturns, market crashes, or sudden changes in market sentiment. These events are not always predictable, and no amount of skill or experience can completely insulate an investor from their effects. When we focus only on successful investors, we may forget that even the best investment strategies can be vulnerable to unforeseen events.

Failure can also result from psychological biases like fear, greed, and herd mentality. While successful investors often exhibit discipline and emotional control, it's important to recognize that not everyone can maintain this level of detachment from their investments. Market risks are magnified when emotions take control, leading to poor decision-making and ultimately, financial loss.

By studying the failures of other investors, we gain insight into how market risks manifest in real-world situations.

We learn that failure is not always the result of bad strategies, but often the outcome of external factors that no one can control. This understanding is crucial for developing a more balanced approach to risk management.

Another problem with focusing solely on successful investors is that it can obscure the hidden risks that lurk beneath the surface of financial markets. Many successful investors may appear to have avoided these risks, but that doesn't mean they don't exist. Hidden risks can include factors like systemic risk, geopolitical events, regulatory changes, and technological disruptions.

Successful investors often have the benefit of hindsight when discussing their strategies. They can point to the risks they successfully navigated, but this does not mean they were always aware of those risks at the time. In many cases, successful investors got lucky, benefiting from market conditions they did not foresee. This can lead others to underestimate the level of uncertainty involved in investing.

Another cognitive bias that contributes to the skewed understanding of market risks is confirmation bias. Confirmation bias refers to the tendency to search for, interpret, and recall information in a way that confirms one's pre-existing beliefs. In investing, confirmation bias often leads people to focus on the success stories that align with their belief in the power of the market or the effectiveness of a particular investment strategy.

When investors look for success stories to validate their own decisions, they may ignore evidence that contradicts their views, such as stories of failure or data suggesting that the market is riskier than they realize. By selectively focusing on the information that supports their decisions, investors can create an illusion of safety and security, which can lead to taking on more risk than they are prepared for.

Confirmation bias also affects how investors process

market data. Investors may ignore negative indicators, focusing only on the positive signals that align with their belief in their chosen strategy. This can lead to a skewed perception of the market's risk, making it appear more favorable than it actually is.

The investment world often perpetuates the idea that certain strategies are "foolproof" if followed correctly. However, by focusing on the successes of those who have employed these strategies, we fail to recognize that there is no surefire way to guarantee returns in the market. Every investment carries risk, and no strategy can completely eliminate the possibility of loss.

One popular example is the value investing strategy championed by Warren Buffet. While value investing has been highly successful for Buffet and others, it has not always produced consistent returns for every investor. The market is constantly changing, and what worked in one era may not work in another. By focusing only on the success stories of value investors, we may overlook the fact that many who followed the same strategy did not achieve the same level of success.

Moreover, the idea that one can perfectly time the market or consistently pick winning stocks is a myth. Even the most successful investors make mistakes, and they often acknowledge that luck plays a significant role in their success. Focusing on those who have consistently succeeded can create the false impression that failure is avoidable if you simply follow the right steps, when in reality, failure is often an inherent part of the investing process.

To gain a more accurate understanding of market risks, it is essential to broaden our perspective beyond the success stories. One way to do this is by studying the full range of investor experiences, including those who failed or underperformed. This helps to provide a more balanced view of the risks involved in investing and can help investors make more informed decisions.

It's also important to recognize that investing is not a zero-sum game where only winners are celebrated. Many investors experience both gains and losses over time, and it is this mixture of outcomes that defines the true nature of market risk. The volatility and unpredictability of the markets mean that even the best strategies are not immune to failure.

Another important step is to study historical market events, such as financial crises and bubbles, to understand how risks can evolve over time. These events provide valuable lessons about how even the most experienced investors can be blindsided by hidden risks. For example, during the dot-com bubble of the late 1990s, many investors were lured into overvalued tech stocks, only to see their portfolios collapse when the bubble burst.

By learning from these events, investors can better prepare themselves for the risks that lie ahead. Rather than focusing solely on success stories, they can develop a more nuanced view of the market that takes into account the potential for failure.

Focusing solely on successful investors can skew our understanding of market risks by creating a biased narrative that downplays the potential for failure. Psychological biases like survivorship bias and confirmation bias further distort our perception of risk, leading to overconfidence and selective information processing. To gain a more accurate understanding of market risks, it is essential to study both the successes and failures of investors, as well as historical market events.

Investing is inherently risky, and no strategy can guarantee success. By acknowledging the role of failure and learning from it, investors can develop a more balanced approach to risk management. This will ultimately lead to more informed decision-making and a healthier understanding of the stock market.

THE QUIET POWER OF DOING NOTHING

When it comes to the stock market, people are often encouraged to take action: buy, sell, rebalance, or adjust their portfolios frequently in response to market news. The constant barrage of information from financial news, social media, and investment newsletters can create a sense of urgency that forces investors to feel like they always need to be doing something. However, there are times when inaction—doing absolutely nothing—can be the best decision an investor makes.

We will explore the counterintuitive idea that inaction can sometimes yield better results than constant activity in the stock market. We'll discuss the psychological, behavioral, and practical reasons why inaction can be a smart strategy. We'll also examine historical examples, the benefits of long-term investing, the pitfalls of overtrading, and how inaction aligns with some of the most successful investment philosophies.

Human beings are wired to act. In times of uncertainty or stress, our natural instinct is to do something to regain control or improve our situation. This tendency extends to the stock market, where the volatility of prices and constant news can make investors feel anxious. Whether the market is rising or falling, it can seem like there is always a reason to make a move—buy to capitalize on gains or sell to avoid losses. This psychological pressure leads many investors to overtrade, making decisions driven by emotion rather than logic.

One of the strongest arguments for inaction in the stock market is the power of long-term investing. Over time, the stock market has historically trended upwards, despite periods of volatility, crashes, and corrections. Investors who buy quality assets and hold them for the long term often benefit from the power of compounding, where returns on an investment generate their own returns over time. This effect accelerates as the investment horizon lengthens.

The most successful investors, such as Warren Buffett, advocate for a long-term approach to investing. Buffett's famous quote, "Our favorite holding period is forever," underscores his belief in the value of inaction. Once an investor has made a well-considered purchase of a strong company with good fundamentals, time, rather than frequent trading, becomes the primary tool for wealth accumulation.

One of the most compelling reasons to advocate for inaction in the stock market is the risk associated with overtrading. Frequent trading, often motivated by a desire to "beat the market," can erode returns in several ways:

Transaction Costs: Every trade comes with a cost, whether it's a commission fee, bid-ask spread, or taxes on capital gains. For investors who make frequent trades, these costs can quickly add up and eat into overall returns. While the rise of commission-free trading platforms has reduced the burden of fees, transaction costs still exist, particularly when it comes to taxes. Inaction, by contrast, avoids these costs entirely.

Market Timing: Attempting to time the market—buying low and selling high—sounds appealing in theory, but it is incredibly difficult to execute successfully over the long term. Markets are unpredictable, and short-term price movements are influenced by countless factors, many of which are beyond the control of investors. Studies have shown that even professional traders struggle to consistently time the market. Missing just a few of the market's best-performing days can dramatically reduce returns. By remaining inactive, investors avoid the risks of poor market timing.

Emotional Decision-Making: Frequent trading is often driven by emotional reactions to market news or price movements. Investors may panic during a downturn and sell, only to buy back in when prices have recovered—effectively buying high and selling low. Inaction prevents these emotionally driven trades and allows investors to stick to a long-term strategy.

Tax Implications: Short-term trades are subject to higher tax rates on capital gains, which can significantly reduce an investor's overall return. By holding investments for the long term, investors can benefit from lower long-term capital gains tax rates. Inaction, therefore, has a direct financial benefit in terms of tax efficiency.

Inaction also allows the magic of compounding to work uninterrupted. Compounding is the process of earning returns not just on the original investment, but also on the returns that investment generates over time. The longer an investor remains invested, the more compounding can accelerate wealth accumulation.

For compounding to work effectively, it requires time and patience. Frequent trading interrupts this process by resetting the investment each time an asset is bought or sold. In contrast, investors who remain inactive and hold their investments for the long term give compounding the time it needs to work its magic.

Consider the case of dividend reinvestment. Many companies pay dividends to their shareholders, and investors who reinvest those dividends benefit from compounding. Over time, reinvested dividends can significantly boost total returns. By doing nothing—simply allowing dividends to be reinvested

—an investor can harness the power of compounding to grow their wealth.

Inaction also allows the magic of compounding to work uninterrupted. Compounding is the process of earning returns not just on the original investment, but also on the returns that investment generates over time. The longer an investor remains invested, the more compounding can accelerate wealth accumulation.

For compounding to work effectively, it requires time and patience. Frequent trading interrupts this process by resetting the investment each time an asset is bought or sold. In contrast, investors who remain inactive and hold their investments for the long term give compounding the time it needs to work its magic.

Consider the case of dividend reinvestment. Many companies pay dividends to their shareholders, and investors who reinvest those dividends benefit from compounding. Over time, reinvested dividends can significantly boost total returns. By doing nothing—simply allowing dividends to be reinvested—an investor can harness the power of compounding to grow their wealth.

Inaction aligns with a long-term investment perspective, which is one of the most reliable ways to generate wealth in the stock market. Markets are inherently volatile in the short term, but they tend to smooth out over longer time horizons. By focusing on the long term, investors can avoid being swayed by short-term noise and volatility.

A long-term perspective also allows investors to take advantage of dollar-cost averaging, a strategy in which they invest a fixed amount of money at regular intervals, regardless of the market's performance. This approach reduces the impact of market timing and allows investors to accumulate shares at various price points. In the long run, dollar-cost averaging helps reduce the average cost per share, leading to better overall returns.

Inaction plays a key role in this strategy. By sticking to a consistent investment plan and resisting the temptation to react to short-term market movements, investors can steadily build wealth over time.

Inaction can also serve as an effective risk management tool. Constantly adjusting a portfolio in response to market movements can introduce unnecessary risks, particularly if those moves are driven by emotion rather than careful analysis. By remaining inactive, investors avoid the risks associated with overtrading and emotional decision-making.

Inaction also prevents investors from reacting impulsively to market noise. Financial news is often sensationalized, with headlines designed to provoke fear or excitement. However, many of these headlines are irrelevant to long-term investors. By ignoring the noise and sticking to a long-term plan, investors can avoid making decisions that might harm their portfolio.

In a world that encourages constant action, doing nothing may seem like a radical approach to investing. However, history and research have shown that inaction can be one of the most powerful tools in an investor's arsenal. By resisting the urge to trade frequently, investors can avoid the pitfalls of overtrading, emotional decision-making, and poor market timing. Inaction allows investors to benefit from the power of compounding, reduce transaction costs, and maintain a long-term perspective.

The key to successful investing is not constant activity, but rather thoughtful inaction. By doing nothing when it's appropriate, investors can give their portfolios the time they need to grow and reach their full potential. Patience, discipline, and a long-term outlook are often the best strategies for achieving lasting success in the stock market.

REVENGE TRADING: THE TRAP OF TRYING TO "WIN BACK" LOSSES

The emotional rollercoaster of investing is something that every investor, no matter how experienced, must contend with. While the highs of a market rally can elicit excitement and confidence, the lows of a downturn or personal financial loss can evoke powerful emotions such as fear, anger, and frustration. These emotional reactions can cloud judgment, leading investors to make decisions that are not aligned with their best long-term interests. In many cases, investors who experience a significant financial loss become more vulnerable to high-risk decisions in a desperate attempt to recover quickly.

This article explores the psychological and emotional factors that lead to poor decision-making after a loss, how losses can trigger high-risk behavior, and the importance of maintaining emotional discipline in investing. We will examine the role of behavioral finance in understanding these patterns, as well as offer strategies for mitigating the emotional impact of losses in order to avoid falling into the trap of high-risk decisions.

Losses, whether financial or otherwise, have a profound psychological impact on human beings. When an investor suffers a loss, their natural instinct is to do something to rectify the situation. This instinct often overrides rational thinking, making it difficult to remain objective and measured. Emotions, such as frustration, fear, and desperation, can push investors into high-risk decisions in the hope of making up for their losses quickly. Rather than accepting the loss as part of the normal ups and downs of investing, the pain can compel them to act impulsively, increasing their exposure to further losses.

To understand how emotions influence high-risk decision-making, it's important to consider the emotional cycle that investors often go through after experiencing a significant loss. This cycle is akin to the stages of grief, where denial, anger, bargaining, depression, and acceptance all play a role in how an investor reacts to losing money.

Denial: Initially, investors may deny the severity of the loss, believing that the market will quickly recover or that their investment was sound despite the downturn. During this stage, they may hold onto a losing position longer than they should, refusing to cut their losses and move on.

Anger: As the loss becomes more apparent, investors may become angry—angry at themselves for making the wrong decision, angry at the market for being unpredictable, or angry at external forces such as economic or political events. Anger can cloud judgment and lead to impulsive decisions, such as making risky trades in an attempt to "get even" with the market.

Bargaining: At this stage, investors may begin to rationalize their losses by engaging in riskier investments in the hope of recovering quickly. They may bargain with themselves, thinking that one big win will make up for the losses. This is often where the transition to high-risk behavior occurs, as the need for quick recovery overrides logical, long-term planning.

Depression: After multiple failed attempts to recover from

a loss, investors may experience feelings of despair or hopelessness. This can lead to further high-risk decisions out of desperation, as they feel they have nothing left to lose.

Acceptance: Finally, some investors reach a point of acceptance, acknowledging the loss as part of the investing process and refocusing on their long-term strategy. However, many investors never reach this stage before making a series of poor decisions that only exacerbate their losses.

Understanding this emotional cycle is critical because it shows how easy it is for investors to fall into high-risk behaviors as they struggle to cope with the pain of a loss. Each stage of the cycle brings its own emotional challenges, and without proper management, these emotions can drive investors toward reckless decision-making.

One of the most common high-risk behaviors after a loss is the urge to double down on risky investments in an attempt to make up for the loss quickly. This behavior, often referred to as loss chasing, is seen in various forms of financial decision-making, including gambling, day trading, and speculative investing.

In the context of investing, loss chasing occurs when an investor, after experiencing a significant loss, increases their risk exposure in the hope of making up for the loss with a big win. This could involve putting more money into a risky stock, investing in highly speculative assets like cryptocurrencies, or trading on margin (borrowing money to invest). The rationale behind this behavior is that a larger, riskier bet has the potential to generate a high return, which would wipe out the previous loss.

After a loss, investors may become more susceptible to FOMO as they desperately seek opportunities to bounce back. The desire to "catch up" or not fall further behind can lead them to chase speculative investments without fully understanding the risks involved. FOMO-driven decisions are often based on hype rather than careful analysis, increasing the likelihood of further losses.

Financial losses are stressful, and stress can impair cognitive function, making it difficult for investors to think clearly and make rational decisions. When under stress, the brain's fight-or-flight response is activated, leading to impulsive behavior and a focus on short-term solutions. This response is useful in situations where immediate action is necessary, such as when faced with a physical threat. However, in the context of investing, this response can lead to poor decisions that exacerbate the problem.

Stress also affects risk tolerance. Under normal circumstances, investors may have a well-defined level of risk they are comfortable with. However, after a loss, the stress of trying to recover may push them to take on more risk than they normally would. This increase in risk tolerance is not based on a careful reassessment of their financial goals but rather on an emotional reaction to the loss.

Financial losses are emotionally taxing, and they have the potential to push investors into making high-risk decisions that can lead to even greater losses. By understanding the psychological and emotional factors that drive this behavior, investors can take steps to mitigate the impact of losses and avoid the pitfalls of impulsive decision-making.

Maintaining emotional discipline is one of the most challenging aspects of investing, but it is also one of the most important. The key to long-term success in the stock market is not to avoid losses altogether, but to manage them in a way that preserves your financial stability and keeps you on track toward your goals. By resisting the urge to chase losses, staying focused on long-term objectives, and managing risk appropriately, investors can avoid the dangerous cycle of high-risk decision-making after a loss.

THE PSYCHOLOGY OF DIVIDENDS: SECURITY IN SMALL GAINS

In times of economic uncertainty, many investors gravitate toward more stable and predictable investment options to weather the storm. One such option that has consistently attracted attention during periods of market volatility is dividend-paying stocks. These stocks offer a form of income through regular cash distributions, providing a sense of security to investors who are wary of the unpredictable price movements that characterize uncertain markets.

Dividend income streams are highly valued by investors for several reasons: they provide consistent returns, they can help mitigate losses during market downturns, and they often signal financial health and stability in the companies issuing them. This article will explore the key factors behind the popularity of dividend income streams in uncertain markets, the psychological comfort dividends provide, and why they are considered a safer bet during times of turbulence.

When market conditions are volatile, investors seek investments that offer some degree of predictability. Dividend-paying stocks meet this need by providing regular cash payouts, regardless of market price fluctuations. For long-term investors, dividends offer a reliable source of income that can cushion the impact of price volatility. Even if the market is falling, the income from dividends can provide investors with a tangible return, which is reassuring when capital gains are difficult to achieve.

Dividends essentially act as a buffer during periods of uncertainty. Even when stock prices decline, dividend income provides a form of compensation, softening the blow of capital losses. This income stream can be particularly attractive to retirees and conservative investors who rely on a steady cash flow to meet their financial needs.

In contrast, growth stocks, which typically do not pay dividends, rely heavily on capital appreciation. While growth stocks may offer substantial long-term returns, their prices can be highly volatile, and they may suffer steep declines during economic downturns. In uncertain markets, investors may prefer the reliability of dividend stocks over the uncertainty of capital appreciation alone.

Another reason investors favor dividend-paying stocks in uncertain markets is that dividends are often viewed as a sign of a company's financial health and stability. Companies that consistently pay dividends, especially those with a long history of doing so, are typically seen as financially strong and well-managed. These companies are often referred to as "blue-chip" stocks and are associated with large, established firms in industries such as consumer goods, utilities, and healthcare.

The ability to pay and maintain dividends during periods of economic difficulty suggests that a company has strong cash flow, prudent financial management, and a stable business model. In times of uncertainty, these qualities become even more important, as investors seek to avoid companies that may be struggling or at risk of bankruptcy.

In fact, many companies make a point of maintaining

or even increasing their dividend payouts during downturns to reassure investors. Cutting or suspending a dividend can be interpreted as a sign of financial distress, which could lead to a sharp decline in the company's stock price. Therefore, companies that are able to continue paying dividends during uncertain times are often perceived as more resilient, making their stocks more attractive to risk-averse investors.

This signaling effect is particularly valuable during market downturns, as it provides investors with a tangible metric by which to judge the stability of a company. For instance, companies that are part of the Dividend Aristocrats—a group of S&P 500 companies that have consistently increased their dividends for at least 25 consecutive years—are often seen as particularly reliable investments in turbulent times.

Dividends are an important component of total return, which includes both capital appreciation (the increase in stock price) and income from dividends. In uncertain markets, capital appreciation can be difficult to achieve, as stock prices may stagnate or decline due to economic or geopolitical instability. During these periods, dividends can account for a larger proportion of total return, providing investors with a form of compensation even when price gains are elusive.

Historically, dividends have made a significant contribution to the total return of stocks over the long term. For example, over the past century, dividends have accounted for a substantial portion of the total return from U.S. equities. In fact, during certain decades, dividends have contributed as much as 40% or more of the total return from stocks.

This role of dividends in total return becomes even more important during bear markets, when stock prices are falling. In such environments, the regular income from dividends can provide a more consistent return than relying on capital gains, which may be negative or minimal. As a result, dividend-paying stocks tend to be less volatile and perform better than non-dividend-paying stocks during downturns.

In addition to providing a stable income stream, reinvesting dividends can further enhance total returns over time. When dividends are reinvested, they purchase additional shares of the stock, which can compound over time and generate even greater returns in the long run. This compounding effect is particularly powerful in uncertain markets, where stock prices may fluctuate but dividends continue to provide a Dividends are an important component of total return, which includes both capital appreciation (the increase in stock price) and income from dividends. In uncertain markets, capital appreciation can be difficult to achieve, as stock prices may stagnate or decline due to economic or geopolitical instability. During these periods, dividends can account for a larger proportion of total return, providing investors with a form of compensation even when price gains are elusive.

Historically, dividends have made a significant contribution to the total return of stocks over the long term. For example, over the past century, dividends have accounted for a substantial portion of the total return from U.S. equities. In fact, during certain decades, dividends have contributed as much as 40% or more of the total return from stocks.

This role of dividends in total return becomes even more important during bear markets, when stock prices are falling. In such environments, the regular income from dividends can provide a more consistent return than relying on capital gains, which may be negative or minimal. As a result, dividend-paying stocks tend to be less volatile and perform better than non-dividend-paying stocks during downturns.

In addition to providing a stable income stream, reinvesting dividends can further enhance total returns over time. When dividends are reinvested, they purchase additional shares of the stock, which can compound over time and generate even greater returns in the long run. This compounding effect is particularly powerful in uncertain markets, where stock prices may fluctuate but dividends continue to provide a steady source of growth.

Dividend-paying stocks are generally considered to be less volatile than their non-dividend-paying counterparts. Companies that pay dividends are often mature, established businesses with more predictable earnings and cash flows. As a result, their stock prices tend to be more stable, particularly during periods of market uncertainty.

Dividend-paying stocks, especially those in sectors like utilities, consumer staples, and healthcare, are often referred to as defensive stocks because they tend to perform better in challenging economic environments. These companies provide essential goods and services that people continue to need regardless of the state of the economy. As a result, their revenues and profits are less sensitive to economic cycles, making them more resilient during downturns.

In contrast, companies in more cyclical sectors, such as technology, energy, or luxury goods, tend to experience greater swings in profitability and stock price during periods of economic uncertainty. These companies may cut back on dividends or halt them altogether during difficult times, making their stocks less appealing to risk-averse investors.

The lower volatility of dividend-paying stocks is particularly important in uncertain markets, where price swings can be extreme and unpredictable. By investing in dividend-paying stocks, investors can reduce the overall volatility of their portfolio, which can help preserve capital and provide a more stable source of returns during periods of market turbulence.

Inflation erodes the purchasing power of money over time, which can be a major concern for investors, especially during periods of rising inflation. In uncertain markets, inflationary pressures may become more pronounced, as central banks and governments implement measures to stimulate the economy, such as low interest rates and quantitative easing.

Dividend-paying stocks can provide a hedge against inflation because many companies that pay dividends, particularly those in defensive sectors, have the ability to raise prices and pass on higher costs to consumers. As a result, their earnings may continue to grow even in an inflationary environment, allowing them to maintain or increase their dividends.

In addition, dividend yields—the annual dividend payout as a percentage of the stock price—can act as a cushion against inflation. For example, if a stock has a dividend yield of 4%, and inflation is running at 2%, the investor is still receiving a positive real return on their investment. In this way, dividend income can help protect against the eroding effects of inflation on the value of an investor's portfolio.

Compared to bonds and other fixed-income investments, which can lose value in a rising inflation environment, dividend-paying stocks offer the potential for both income and capital appreciation. While the fixed interest payments on bonds may become less valuable as inflation rises, companies that can grow their earnings and dividends provide a more attractive investment option in uncertain, inflationary markets.

Beyond the financial benefits of dividend-paying stocks, dividends also provide a psychological comfort to investors during uncertain times. Behavioral finance, a field that studies how psychological factors influence financial decision-making, helps explain why investors may prefer dividend-paying stocks during periods of market volatility.

One key concept from behavioral finance is mental accounting, which suggests that people tend to separate their investments into different mental "accounts" based on their purpose or source of return. For example, investors may view dividend income as a separate stream of cash flow that is less tied to the stock's price movements. Even if the stock's price fluctuates, the dividend payments provide a sense of stability and control, which can help investors feel more secure during uncertain markets.

Dividends also play into the endowment effect, where people place a higher value on assets they already own. Receiving regular dividend payments can create a sense of ownership and attachment to the stock, making investors less likely to sell during periods of market turbulence. This behavior can help prevent emotional, short-term decisions and encourage a longer-term investment approach.

Additionally, dividends provide a tangible return that can help satisfy the human need for immediate rewards. Investors are often tempted to focus on short-term gains, especially in volatile markets. Dividends offer a way to receive consistent, near-term income without having to sell shares, which can help reduce the temptation to make impulsive trades during uncertain times.

Interest rates play a significant role in determining the attractiveness of dividend-paying stocks. When interest rates are low, as they often are during periods of economic uncertainty, the yields on bonds and other fixed-income investments are also low. This makes dividend-paying stocks, with their potential for higher yields and capital appreciation, more appealing to income-seeking investors.

During times of economic downturn or recession, central banks may lower interest rates to stimulate growth. In such an environment, the yields on government bonds, savings accounts, and other traditional income-generating assets may fall below the dividend yields offered by certain stocks. As a result, investors seeking reliable income may turn to dividend-paying stocks as a more attractive alternative.

Moreover, in a low-interest-rate environment, the spread between dividend yields and bond yields becomes a crucial consideration. If dividend yields are significantly higher than bond yields, dividend-paying stocks may be seen as a better option for income-focused investors. Conversely, when interest rates rise, the relative attractiveness of dividend stocks may diminish as bond yields increase.

In uncertain markets, where economic growth is slow and interest rates are low, the appeal of dividend-paying stocks is magnified, as they offer a combination of income and potential price appreciation that is difficult to find in other asset classes.

In uncertain markets, the importance of stability, predictability, and income becomes paramount for investors. Dividend-paying stocks provide a reliable income stream, reduce portfolio volatility, and offer a hedge against inflation, making them an attractive option during periods of economic turbulence. By signaling financial health, contributing to total returns, and offering psychological comfort, dividends give investors a sense of security in times when market prices may be highly volatile.

For these reasons, dividend income streams will likely continue to play a critical role in the portfolios of investors who seek to navigate the challenges of uncertain markets. Whether through blue-chip stocks with a long history of stable payouts or defensive stocks in recession-resistant industries, dividends offer a time-tested way for investors to preserve their wealth and achieve their financial goals in an ever-changing market environment.

MANAGING EXPECTATIONS: THE KEY TO INVESTOR HAPPINESS

The stock market is often portrayed as a fast track to wealth, with stories of investors making millions from well-timed trades and seemingly endless opportunities for profit. This portrayal, however, can set unrealistic expectations for investors, leading to disappointment, frustration, and even financial loss when their investments do not live up to these idealized outcomes.

Setting realistic expectations is crucial for long-term success in the stock market. It helps investors make more informed decisions, reduces emotional responses to short-term market fluctuations, and ultimately leads to more satisfying investment experiences. In this article, we will explore why managing expectations is so important, how unrealistic expectations can lead to poor decision-making, and the steps investors can take to align their goals with reality for a more rewarding journey in the stock market.

The first step to achieving a satisfying investment

experience is to understand that the stock market is inherently unpredictable. Prices fluctuate daily, and it is impossible to consistently time the market or predict with certainty how individual stocks will perform in the short term. Without a clear understanding of this, investors may set themselves up for failure by expecting quick, outsized returns, which is often unrealistic.

By setting realistic expectations, investors can shift their focus from trying to achieve rapid wealth to building long-term financial success. This approach fosters patience and discipline, two qualities that are essential for navigating the ups and downs of the stock market. Importantly, it helps investors avoid impulsive actions based on short-term market movements, such as panic selling during a downturn or chasing after high-flying stocks that may be overvalued.

Moreover, realistic expectations provide a more grounded perspective on risk and reward. Investors who understand the average returns of different asset classes, and the time frames over which these returns are likely to materialize, are better equipped to handle the emotional aspects of investing. This mindset encourages them to stay invested through market volatility, leading to better long-term outcomes and a more positive investment experience overall.

One of the biggest pitfalls for investors is entering the stock market with unrealistic expectations. Many new investors, influenced by stories of rapid gains or media hype around certain stocks, may expect to double or triple their money in a short time. When these expectations are not met, it can lead to frustration and disappointment, causing them to abandon their investment strategy prematurely.

The idea of getting rich quickly through the stock market is enticing, but it is also one of the most dangerous misconceptions. Investing is not a guaranteed shortcut to wealth, and expecting quick, exponential growth often leads investors to take on excessive risks in search of higher returns. This risk-chasing behavior can backfire, especially in volatile markets or when investing in speculative stocks. When these high-risk bets do not pay off, investors may lose significant amounts of money, which can lead to disillusionment and the abandonment of investing altogether.

Market timing, trying to buy low and sell high at exactly the right moments, is a strategy that even the most experienced investors struggle with. However, many novice investors overestimate their ability to predict market movements and end up making costly mistakes. They may sell during a downturn, locking in losses, or buy during a rally, only to see the stock price fall afterward. Setting realistic expectations about the difficulty of timing the market can prevent investors from making these types of impulsive decisions.

Another common misconception is that stock prices will rise steadily over time. In reality, the stock market is cyclical, with periods of both growth and decline. Investors who expect constant upward growth may panic during market corrections or bear markets, which are natural parts of the market cycle. Those with unrealistic expectations may feel compelled to sell when prices drop, missing out on potential gains when the market eventually recovers.

Unrealistic expectations often go hand-in-hand with underestimating the risks involved in investing. Some investors may believe that they can achieve high returns with minimal risk, leading them to over-concentrate their portfolio in a few high-risk assets. When these investments underperform, the losses can be devastating. Setting realistic expectations involves understanding that all investments carry some level of risk, and that diversification is key to managing this risk.

Setting realistic expectations is one of the most important factors in achieving a satisfying investment experience in the stock market. By understanding the historical performance of the market, embracing the importance of diversification, and aligning investment strategies with personal goals, investors can develop a more balanced and informed approach to investing.

Realistic expectations help investors navigate the emotional challenges of stock market volatility, reduce the likelihood of impulsive decision-making, and foster a long-term mindset that is essential for building wealth. In the end, the satisfaction that comes from steady, disciplined investing far outweighs the disappointment of chasing unrealistic gains.

Investors who take the time to set realistic expectations will not only enjoy a more rewarding investment journey, but they will also be better positioned to achieve their financial goals with confidence and peace of mind.

THE EMOTIONAL COST OF OVERTRADING

The stock market is often seen as a realm of opportunity, a place where fortunes can be made, or lost, in an instant. For many investors, the thrill of trading can quickly turn into an obsession, leading to a phenomenon known as overtrading. While the financial implications of overtrading are widely discussed, the emotional costs associated with this behavior are less frequently acknowledged yet can be equally detrimental. This section explores the emotional toll of overtrading, its psychological underpinnings.

Overtrading refers to the excessive buying and selling of stocks, often driven by impulsive decision-making rather than a well-thought-out strategy. This behavior can stem from various factors, including the desire for quick profits, the influence of market trends, or the emotional highs and lows associated with trading.

Investors who overtrade may not only incur higher transaction costs but also expose themselves to significant emotional stress. The thrill of making a trade can quickly devolve into anxiety and regret, particularly when market fluctuations lead to unexpected losses. Understanding the emotional cost of overtrading is essential for any investor looking to navigate the stock market effectively.

Emotional turmoil caused by overtrading can impair an investor's ability to make sound decisions. When overwhelmed by anxiety, regret, or guilt, individuals may become reactive rather than analytical, making trades based on impulse rather than research or strategy. This decline in decision-making quality can lead to further losses, reinforcing negative emotions and perpetuating the cycle of overtrading.

Emotions can cloud judgment, making it difficult to adhere to a well-thought-out investment strategy. As a result, overtraders may find themselves engaging in behaviors that are counterproductive to their long-term financial goals.

Overtrading can take a toll on an investor's self-esteem. Frequent losses, compounded by the emotional strain of trading, can lead individuals to question their abilities and knowledge. This erosion of self-confidence can create a vicious cycle, where low self-esteem leads to further impulsive trades in an attempt to prove oneself or recover losses.

The struggle to maintain a sense of competence and control can be exhausting, leading to withdrawal from the market altogether or a complete disengagement from investing.

The constant pressure and emotional strain associated with overtrading can lead to burnout, where investors become mentally and emotionally exhausted from the relentless cycle of trading. This burnout can result in a withdrawal from investing altogether, as individuals feel overwhelmed and unable to cope with the demands of the market.

Withdrawal from investing can lead to a missed opportunity for long-term wealth building. Those who once engaged actively in the stock market may find themselves disengaged, forfeiting the potential benefits of investing over time.

The emotional toll of overtrading can spill over into personal relationships. Increased stress, anxiety, and frustration can lead to irritability and withdrawal from loved ones. Family and friends may notice changes in behavior, leading to conflicts and misunderstandings.

Financial stress resulting from overtrading can strain relationships. The emotional burden of financial losses can create tension and conflict between partners, as differing investment philosophies and risk tolerances come to the forefront. The need to prioritize emotional well-being in investing extends beyond the individual, impacting those closest to them.

Overtrading can lead to significant emotional costs that affect both mental well-being and financial stability. The psychological drivers behind overtrading, including the thrill of the game, fear of missing out, loss aversion, and overconfidence, can create a vicious cycle of stress, regret, and impulsive decision-making.

The emotional toll of overtrading, manifesting as anxiety, regret, impaired decision-making, and low self-esteem, can have long-lasting consequences, both financially and personally. Recognizing these emotional costs is essential for investors seeking a balanced and fulfilling investment experience.

Understanding the emotional costs of overtrading empowers investors to take control of their trading behavior, fostering a more rewarding and satisfying investment experience in the long run.

THE FEAR OF RECESSION: NAVIGATING THROUGH ECONOMIC DOWNTURNS

Economic recessions can be challenging periods for investors, characterized by market volatility, reduced consumer spending, and increased uncertainty. During such times, many investors may feel anxious, overwhelmed, or compelled to make impulsive decisions that can adversely impact their financial well-being. However, psychological preparation can significantly mitigate the negative effects of a recession, enabling investors to not only survive but also thrive in challenging economic environments. This article explores the psychological strategies and techniques investors can adopt to enhance their resilience, maintain a positive mindset, and make informed decisions during recessions.

Psychological preparation equips investors with the tools to manage their emotions and make sound decisions during recessions. By fostering a proactive mindset and employing strategies to strengthen mental resilience, investors can navigate economic downturns more effectively.

A resilient mindset is characterized by adaptability, optimism, and the ability to learn from setbacks. Developing this mindset can help investors maintain a positive outlook during challenging times.

Adaptability: Being open to change and willing to adjust strategies in response to evolving market conditions can enhance resilience. Investors should recognize that recessions are part of the economic cycle and that recovery will eventually follow.

Optimism: Cultivating a sense of optimism can help counteract fear and anxiety. Focus on potential opportunities that may arise during recessions, such as undervalued assets or companies with strong fundamentals.

Learning from Setbacks: Embrace failures as learning opportunities. Analyzing past investment decisions can provide valuable insights and enhance future decision-making.

Maintaining a balanced perspective is essential for preventing emotional decision-making during recessions. Remind yourself that recessions are temporary and that markets historically recover over time. Keeping a long-term perspective can help mitigate the emotional impact of short-term fluctuations.

Recognize that feeling anxious or fearful during a recession is natural. Instead of suppressing these emotions, acknowledge them and allow yourself to process them without letting them dictate your decisions. While recessions pose challenges, they can also present unique investment opportunities. Recognizing and capitalizing on these opportunities requires psychological preparation and a proactive mindset.

During economic downturns, many stocks and

assets may become undervalued due to market panic. A psychologically prepared investor can identify these opportunities and make informed investment decisions.

Conduct Thorough Research: Analyze companies with strong fundamentals, robust balance sheets, and resilient business models. Investing in quality assets during a recession can lead to significant long-term gains when the market recovers.

Consider Dollar-Cost Averaging: Employ dollar-cost averaging by consistently investing a fixed amount in the market, regardless of its current condition. This strategy can help reduce the impact of volatility and take advantage of lower prices during a recession.

Defensive stocks, such as utilities, consumer staples, and healthcare companies, tend to perform relatively well during recessions. These sectors are less sensitive to economic downturns as they provide essential goods and services.

Focus on Stability: Investing in defensive stocks can help mitigate losses during market downturns, providing a buffer against volatility.

Assess Dividend Yield: Companies that maintain stable dividends during recessions can offer a source of income and enhance portfolio stability.

Psychological preparation is essential for investors seeking to navigate the challenges posed by economic recessions successfully. By understanding the psychological impacts of recessions, building resilience, and employing effective strategies, investors can enhance their ability to make informed decisions and capitalize on opportunities.

ADAPTING TO CHANGE: MENTAL FLEXIBILITY IN THE MARKET

In the world of investing and finance, the ability to adapt to rapidly changing market conditions is paramount. Psychological agility—defined as the capacity to swiftly and effectively adapt one's thoughts, emotions, and behaviors in response to changing circumstances—is crucial for investors. This concept goes beyond simple flexibility; it encompasses resilience, emotional intelligence, and a proactive mindset. As markets fluctuate due to various factors such as economic data releases, geopolitical events, or shifts in investor sentiment, those who possess psychological agility are better equipped to navigate uncertainties, capitalize on opportunities, and manage risks. This article delves into why psychological agility is essential for investors in today's dynamic market environment.

Before exploring the significance of psychological agility, it's essential to understand the nature of market dynamics. Markets are influenced by a multitude of factors that can cause rapid shifts in direction, including:

Economic indicators such as GDP growth, unemployment rates, inflation, and consumer confidence play a crucial role in shaping market sentiment. Investors need to interpret these indicators correctly and adjust their strategies accordingly.

Geopolitical events, such as elections, trade negotiations, and conflicts, can lead to sudden market fluctuations. These events can create uncertainty and volatility, making it necessary for investors to respond quickly to changing conditions.

The rise of technology has transformed market dynamics, enabling high-frequency trading and the instantaneous dissemination of information. This rapid exchange of data can lead to swift price movements, requiring investors to remain agile in their decision-making.

Market sentiment can shift dramatically based on news, rumors, or social media trends. Understanding and responding to investor psychology is crucial for making informed investment decisions.

Psychological agility encompasses several key components that enhance an investor's ability to respond to changing market conditions effectively.

Emotional intelligence refers to the ability to recognize, understand, and manage one's emotions and the emotions of others. Investors with high emotional intelligence can remain calm and composed during market turbulence, allowing them to make rational decisions rather than impulsive ones.

Self-Regulation: Investors must manage their emotions, especially fear and greed. For example, during market downturns, emotionally intelligent investors can resist the urge to sell out of panic, enabling them to stick to their long-term strategies.

Empathy: Understanding the emotions of others can provide insights into market trends. For instance, recognizing when the market is overly optimistic or pessimistic can help investors position themselves accordingly.

Cognitive flexibility refers to the mental ability to switch between thinking about different concepts or to think about multiple concepts simultaneously. This trait is essential for adapting investment strategies to align with evolving market conditions.

Reassessing Strategies: Markets are dynamic; thus, strategies that were effective in the past may not yield the same results in the future. Investors must be willing to reassess their approaches and pivot when necessary.

Exploring New Information: Cognitive flexibility enables investors to seek out and consider new information that may challenge their existing beliefs or strategies. This open-mindedness is crucial for making informed decisions in volatile environments.

Resilience is the capacity to recover quickly from difficulties. In investing, resilience allows individuals to withstand losses and setbacks without losing sight of their long-term goals.

Learning from Failures: Resilient investors view setbacks as learning experiences. For example, if an investment fails, they analyze what went wrong and adjust their strategies accordingly rather than succumbing to defeat.

Maintaining Perspective: Resilience helps investors maintain a long-term perspective, preventing short-term market fluctuations from derailing their overall strategies.

Psychological agility offers numerous advantages for investors, particularly in responding to shifting market dynamics.

Psychological agility improves decision-making by enabling investors to process information more effectively and respond to market changes with confidence.

Reduced Impulsivity: By fostering emotional regulation and self-awareness, investors can reduce impulsive decision-making that often occurs during periods of stress.

Informed Choices: Agility allows investors to analyze market trends, assess risks, and make informed choices based on a comprehensive understanding of their investments.

In a rapidly changing market environment, adaptability is crucial. Psychological agility equips investors with the tools to pivot when necessary.

Flexibility in Strategies: Investors can adapt their strategies in response to new information or changing market conditions, maximizing opportunities for profit while minimizing risk.

Innovative Thinking: Agility encourages innovative thinking, allowing investors to explore alternative investment strategies or asset classes when traditional approaches may no longer be effective.

Psychological agility enhances an investor's ability to manage risk effectively. By maintaining a balanced perspective, investors can assess risks more accurately.

Proactive Risk Assessment: Agility enables investors to identify potential risks early and develop contingency plans to mitigate those risks.

Staying Disciplined: In the face of market volatility, psychologically agile investors are better able to adhere to their risk management strategies, reducing the likelihood of making impulsive, high-risk decisions.

While some individuals may naturally possess psychological agility, it is also a skill that can be developed over time. Here are several strategies to enhance psychological agility:

Investors should commit to lifelong learning, staying informed about market trends, economic indicators, and investment strategies.

Reading and Research: Regularly consume financial news, academic research, and investment literature to expand knowledge and awareness.

Attending Workshops and Seminars: Engage in professional development opportunities that focus on investment strategies, market analysis, and psychological resilience.

Mindfulness techniques can improve emotional regulation and cognitive flexibility, essential components of psychological agility.

Mindfulness Meditation: Practicing mindfulness meditation can enhance self-awareness and promote a sense of calm during market fluctuations.

Journaling: Keeping a journal to reflect on emotions and decision-making processes can help investors identify patterns and areas for improvement.

Receiving feedback from peers, mentors, or financial advisors can provide valuable insights into one's investment strategies and decision-making processes.

Peer Discussions: Engaging in discussions with fellow investors can help clarify thoughts and reveal different perspectives.

Professional Guidance: Consulting with financial advisors can provide expert insights and help investors refine their strategies based on market dynamics.

In an era of rapid change and uncertainty, psychological agility is a crucial asset for investors. The ability to adapt one's thoughts, emotions, and behaviors in response to shifting market dynamics can significantly impact investment success. By cultivating emotional intelligence, cognitive flexibility, and resilience, investors can enhance their decision-making processes, improve adaptability, and manage risks more effectively.

Developing psychological agility requires continuous learning, mindfulness practices, and seeking feedback from peers and mentors. Real-world examples of successful investors like Warren Buffett, Ray Dalio, and Cathie Wood demonstrate the transformative power of psychological agility in navigating complex market dynamics.

Embracing psychological agility can empower investors to thrive in uncertain environments, turning challenges into opportunities and ensuring long-term financial success. In a world where market dynamics can change at a moment's notice, the ability to respond with agility and confidence is an invaluable skill for any investor.

TAMING IMPULSIVITY: HOW TO CONTROL RASH DECISIONS

Investing in the stock market can be both exhilarating and nerve-wracking. The allure of quick profits can sometimes lead to impulsive decisions driven by short-term emotions, such as fear, greed, or anxiety. These impulsive actions often result in significant financial losses and frustration. Therefore, mastering techniques to resist these emotional impulses is essential for achieving long-term investment success. This article will explore various strategies and techniques that investors can use to maintain emotional discipline and make rational decisions, ultimately fostering a more satisfying investment experience.

Creating a robust investment plan is the foundation for resisting impulsive decisions. A well-structured plan outlines specific goals, strategies, and risk tolerance levels, providing a roadmap that investors can follow, regardless of market fluctuations.

The first step in establishing an investment plan is defining clear, measurable financial goals. Goals can range from retirement savings and funding education to purchasing a home or building wealth over time. By articulating these objectives, investors create a sense of purpose that can help guide their decision-making processes.

Time horizons refer to the duration an investor plans to hold their investments. Different time horizons necessitate different strategies and risk levels. By clearly defining time horizons, investors can develop patience and reduce the impulse to react to short-term market movements.

A well-defined trading strategy can significantly reduce impulsive market decisions by establishing clear guidelines for buying and selling.

Establishing specific criteria for entering and exiting trades can help eliminate emotional factors from the decision-making process. Consider the following components when creating trading rules:

Entry Points: Determine specific price levels or technical indicators that will signal a good time to buy. This might include price thresholds, moving averages, or technical patterns.

Exit Points: Define clear exit strategies, including profit-taking levels and stop-loss orders, to protect against losses.

Diversification: Incorporate diversification rules into your strategy to spread risk across various assets, reducing the impact of a single investment on your overall portfolio.

Adherence to a well-defined trading strategy is crucial, even during turbulent market conditions. To maintain discipline:

Document Your Strategy: Write down your trading strategy and refer to it frequently. A documented plan serves as a constant reminder of your objectives and can help keep emotions in check.

Regularly Review and Adjust: Periodically reassess your strategy to ensure it aligns with your goals and risk tolerance. However, avoid making adjustments based solely on short-term market fluctuations.

Limit Emotional Trading: Create a "cooling-off" period before making significant changes to your strategy or portfolio. This delay can help mitigate impulsive decisions made in the heat of the moment.

Mindfulness practices can empower investors to recognize and manage their emotions effectively, reducing impulsive decision-making.

Regular self-reflection is a valuable tool for understanding emotional triggers and how they influence trading behavior. Consider maintaining a trading journal to record your thoughts, feelings, and decisions related to each trade. This practice can help identify patterns in your emotional responses and provide insights into your decision-making process.

Identify Triggers: Recognize specific events or situations that provoke emotional responses, such as market downturns or significant news headlines.

Assess Reactions: Analyze how your emotional state impacts your trading decisions. Reflecting on past trades can help you recognize when emotions influenced your choices.

Engaging in mindfulness techniques can enhance emotional regulation and awareness:

Meditation: Practicing mindfulness meditation can help calm the mind and promote a more balanced emotional state. Even short, daily meditation sessions can cultivate greater awareness of your thoughts and feelings.

Deep Breathing Exercises: Utilize deep breathing exercises during stressful market moments. Focusing on your breath can help ground you and reduce anxiety, allowing for clearer thinking.

Visualization: Visualize your trading goals and the ideal

responses to market fluctuations. This mental rehearsal can help you prepare for emotional challenges and reinforce a calm approach.

Developing effective emotion regulation strategies can further enhance your ability to resist impulsive decisions:

Cognitive Reappraisal: Practice reframing negative thoughts and emotions associated with market volatility. For instance, instead of viewing a market decline as a loss, see it as an opportunity to purchase undervalued assets.

Positive Affirmations: Use positive affirmations to bolster your confidence and resilience in the face of market challenges. Remind yourself of your long-term goals and the importance of sticking to your plan.

Establishing limits on trading activity can help mitigate impulsive decisions driven by emotions.

Limiting the number of trades you make within a specific timeframe can help curb impulsivity. This approach encourages patience and reduces the temptation to react quickly to market fluctuations.

Daily/Weekly Limits: Set a maximum number of trades you will execute each day or week. This limit allows you to focus on the quality of trades rather than the quantity.

Minimum Holding Period: Implement a minimum holding period for investments, such as committing to holding a stock for at least six months before considering a sale. This approach discourages knee-jerk reactions to short-term market movements.

Using stop-loss orders can serve as a safety net against excessive losses while allowing you to stick to your trading strategy.

Define Stop-Loss Levels: Determine a percentage or dollar amount at which you will sell a stock to prevent further losses. This preemptive measure removes the emotional element from the decision to cut losses.

Review Stop-Loss Orders Regularly: Periodically reassess your stop-loss orders to ensure they align with your evolving investment strategy and risk tolerance.

Engaging with a community of like-minded investors can provide valuable emotional support and accountability.

Participating in investment groups or online forums can help you connect with others who share similar interests and goals. Sharing experiences, challenges, and successes can foster a sense of camaraderie and support.

Learn from Others: Engaging in discussions with fellow investors can provide insights into different strategies and approaches, enhancing your understanding of market dynamics.

Seek Accountability: Having a support network can encourage you to stick to your investment plan. Accountability partners can help you remain focused and disciplined during times of emotional turbulence.

Openly discussing your trading experiences, both successes and failures, can help normalize the emotional challenges associated with investing.

Reflect Together: Engaging in collective reflection on trading experiences can provide valuable learning opportunities and foster resilience within the community.

Celebrate Successes: Acknowledging and celebrating each other's successes can create a positive environment, reinforcing the value of disciplined investing.

Continuous education is vital for building confidence and resilience in the face of market fluctuations.

Keeping up-to-date with market trends, economic indicators, and investment strategies can enhance your understanding of market dynamics, enabling you to make more informed decisions.

Read Financial News: Regularly read reputable financial news sources and research reports to stay informed about market developments.

Follow Expert Analysis: Listening to podcasts or attending webinars hosted by experienced investors or financial experts can provide valuable insights.

Reflecting on past trading mistakes can help you identify emotional patterns and improve your decision-making in the future.

Analyze Past Trades: Review both successful and unsuccessful trades to understand what influenced your decisions. Consider how emotions played a role in each scenario.

Adjust Your Strategy: Use the lessons learned from past mistakes to refine your trading strategy and avoid similar pitfalls in the future.

Taking breaks from the market can help you regain perspective and reduce emotional strain.

If you find yourself feeling overwhelmed or anxious, consider stepping away from trading platforms for a period. This break can help clear your mind and allow you to return with a fresh perspective.

Schedule Downtime: Plan regular breaks from trading, whether it's a few hours, days, or even weeks, to recharge and reflect on your strategy.

Engage in Other Activities: Use this time to engage in activities unrelated to investing, such as exercising, spending time with family, or pursuing hobbies.

During breaks, take the opportunity to reassess your financial goals, risk tolerance, and overall investment strategy. This reflection can help you return to the market with renewed focus and discipline.

Resisting impulsive market decisions driven by short-term emotions is crucial for achieving long-term investment success. By establishing a clear investment plan, developing a disciplined trading strategy, practicing mindfulness, setting trading limits, fostering a supportive community, continuously educating oneself, and taking breaks when needed, investors can cultivate emotional resilience and enhance their decision-making processes.

Investing is a journey filled with ups and downs, and understanding the emotional dynamics at play is essential for navigating the complexities of the stock market. By implementing these techniques, investors can minimize impulsive actions and make more rational, informed decisions that align with their financial goals. Ultimately, cultivating emotional discipline is a key factor in fostering a fulfilling and successful investing experience.

CONCLUSION

As we close this exploration of stock market psychology, it's essential to recognize that investing is not merely a numbers game; it is a deeply human endeavor influenced by emotions, biases, and cognitive processes. Understanding the psychological factors that drive market behavior can empower investors to make informed decisions, mitigate risks, and achieve their financial goals. Throughout this book, we have delved into various aspects of stock market psychology, from the emotional responses that arise during periods of volatility to the cognitive biases that can cloud judgment and lead to costly mistakes.

In this conclusion, we will synthesize the key insights discussed in the book and emphasize the importance of integrating psychological awareness into investment strategies. We will also explore the implications of stock market psychology for both individual investors and the broader financial community, underscoring the necessity of fostering a psychologically informed approach to investing.

At its core, investing is a reflection of human behavior. Market dynamics are shaped by the collective actions and reactions of investors, driven by their perceptions, emotions, and biases. This fundamental truth underscores the importance of psychological awareness in investing. Recognizing that markets are not merely driven by economic data but also by the sentiments of participants allows investors to better navigate the complexities of market behavior.

Throughout the book, we examined how emotions such as fear, greed, and anxiety significantly influence decision-making processes. The stock market is often characterized by volatility and uncertainty, and these emotions can lead to impulsive actions that deviate from rational investment strategies.

The fear of losing money can drive investors to make hasty decisions, such as panic selling during market downturns. Understanding the psychological roots of fear can help investors develop strategies to manage their emotions, such as setting predetermined exit points and maintaining a long-term perspective.

The allure of potential gains can lead to overconfidence and excessive risk-taking. Investors must recognize the signs of overconfidence bias and adopt practices such as regular self-assessment and diversification to mitigate these risks.

Cognitive biases play a pivotal role in shaping investment decisions, often leading to suboptimal outcomes. From confirmation bias to anchoring and herd behavior, these biases can distort perceptions and cloud judgment.

By becoming aware of common cognitive biases, investors can develop strategies to counteract their effects. For instance, engaging in critical self-reflection, seeking diverse perspectives, and relying on data-driven analysis can help mitigate the impact of biases on decision-making.

Continuous education about behavioral finance and cognitive biases can empower investors to make more rational decisions. Workshops, reading materials, and discussions with knowledgeable peers can enhance awareness and understanding of psychological factors influencing market behavior.

Adopting a growth-oriented mindset is essential for

achieving long-term investment success. A growth mindset fosters resilience, adaptability, and a willingness to learn from failures.

Investing is fraught with challenges and uncertainties. Investors with a growth mindset view these challenges as opportunities for growth and learning rather than insurmountable obstacles. This perspective encourages individuals to seek innovative solutions and remain open to new strategies.

Every investor will inevitably face setbacks and losses. Those with a growth mindset understand that mistakes are part of the learning process. By analyzing past decisions, identifying areas for improvement, and adjusting strategies accordingly, investors can cultivate a sense of resilience that enhances their long-term performance.

Effective emotional regulation is a cornerstone of successful investing. The ability to manage emotions and maintain composure during periods of market volatility can distinguish successful investors from those who struggle to achieve their goals.

Incorporating mindfulness practices into daily routines can enhance emotional regulation. Mindfulness meditation, for example, helps investors cultivate self-awareness and develop a sense of calm, enabling them to make thoughtful decisions even in turbulent market conditions.

Investors should adopt stress management techniques to cope with the emotional demands of investing. Techniques such as deep breathing exercises, physical activity, and regular breaks from market monitoring can help reduce stress levels and promote a balanced perspective.

Investing can often feel isolating, especially during periods of market turmoil. Building a supportive network of like-minded individuals can provide valuable emotional and intellectual support.

Engaging with fellow investors can foster a sense of community and shared understanding. Participating in investment clubs, online forums, or discussion groups can facilitate the exchange of ideas, strategies, and experiences, enriching the overall investing journey.

Seeking guidance from financial advisors or coaches can also provide valuable insights and support. A professional can offer objective perspectives, help navigate emotional challenges, and assist in developing personalized investment strategies aligned with individual goals.

The principles of stock market psychology extend beyond individual investors; they have significant implications for the broader financial ecosystem. Understanding the psychological dynamics at play can help market participants and institutions foster healthier market behavior.

As we conclude this exploration of stock market psychology, it is essential to recognize that successful investing is not solely about mastering technical analysis or developing complex algorithms; it is fundamentally about understanding the human elements at play. By embracing psychological awareness, investors can navigate the challenges of the market with greater confidence and resilience.

In a world where markets are increasingly influenced by human behavior, cultivating psychological agility is paramount. The lessons gleaned from this book serve as a reminder that investing is a journey, one that requires continuous learning, self-reflection, and a commitment to understanding the emotional and cognitive factors that shape our decisions.

The principles of stock market psychology can empower investors to make informed choices, manage risks effectively, and achieve their financial objectives. By integrating psychological awareness into investment strategies, we can navigate the complexities of the stock market with greater insight, fostering a more sustainable and rewarding investing experience. As we move forward, let us commit to becoming not only better investors but also more psychologically attuned individuals, capable of thriving in the dynamic and often unpredictable world of finance.

www.ingramcontent.com/pod-product-compliance
Lightning Source LLC
Chambersburg PA
CBHW071454220526
45472CB00003B/796